Shepherd's Pie

Other books by Fr. Roberts

PLAYBOY TO PRIEST
Our Sunday Visitor Publishing

YOU BETTER BELIEVE IT
Our Sunday Visitor Publishing

PRAY IT AGAIN, SAM
Our Sunday Visitor Publishing

MARY, THE PERFECT PRAYER PARTNER
Our Sunday Visitor Publishing

PROUD TO BE CATHOLIC
Our Sunday Visitor Publishing

THE REST OF THE WEEK
Pax Tapes

UP ON THE MOUNTAIN
Paraclete Press

For audio and video tapes by Fr. Roberts,
write to Pax Tapes, Inc.

Shepherd's Pie

Father Kenneth J. Roberts

with

Anna Marie Waters

PAX TAPES, INC.

Scripture references: THE NEW AMERICAN BIBLE.
Previously published articles are reproduced with the
permission of MEDJUGORJE MAGAZINE and
THE CHICAGO MARIAN CENTER

SHEPHERD'S PIE

first printing, August 1995

PAX TAPES, INC.
P. O. Box 1059
Florissant, Missouri 63031

Library of Congress Card Number: 95-070368
International Standard Book Number: 0-9610984-4-9

Printed in the United States of America

from the Author...

For those of you who are not familiar with English cooking, perhaps the name, SHEPHERD'S PIE doesn't mean anything. But for those of you who are familiar with the dish, you will know that shepherd's pie is really a quite popular entree in many homes in England and throughout the British Isles.

In our home, it was served quite often and we all liked the dish. My mother knew how to make everything appealing, even leftovers. Although most recipes call for chopped meat mixed with onions and gravy, then topped with potatoes, Mum always used our leftover Sunday roast beef. It was a great way to serve up Sunday's fare in a new way. Actually, it wasn't until I was older that I realized she used the leftovers but it didn't matter because we all thought it was delicious.

I really couldn't come up with a more appropriate title for this book than SHEPHERD'S PIE, because it very much resembles Mum's dish. You see, I've taken many of the articles that I've written and have been published over the past several years, and used them for this manuscript. I also decided to take the advice of several of my friends who have suggested that I put together a book of some of the recipes that I have prepared when they invited me to cook a meal for them in their homes. That's a little hobby of mine...I really love to cook. Though I don't often have the time or the opportunity, I'm always grateful when a few close friends indulge me.

So, what you are about to read in the following pages are *leftover* articles that I've written and some of my favorite recipes at the end of the book. Very much like the dish. A little of this and a little of that, all dressed up in a new package...just like Mum's shepherd's pie.

I also invited Anna Marie Waters to include a few of her articles that have been published in the *DEAR CHILDREN* periodical. She maintains that the only reason this invitation was extended was because I asked her to measure ingredients for me for these dishes. I wasn't sure if I used a cup or three-quarters cup, a teaspoon full or a tablespoon full, so she followed me through the kitchen, filled up a bunch of containers with the appropriate ingredients for the dish, recorded how much I used and the end result was a real recipe!

Ann knows her way around a kitchen pretty well since she has five children and eleven grandchildren. Butch, Ann's husband and my best friend, has been gracious enough to be the official taster...with some help from my secretary, Judy Horvath.

Ann knows her way around a word-processor too. She has been typing my manuscripts all the way back to PLAYBOY TO PRIEST which incidentally, was composed, typed and edited on Ann's dining room table. But back then, I wrote in longhand and Ann typed it on an old upright Underwood typewriter.

Though I'm grateful to Ann for measuring all the ingredients, I still would have invited her to contribute some of her articles for this book.

She has been critiquing my writing for twenty seven years and I believe her work will add to this work.

This has been a fun book, not that the subject matter in the articles are not serious. On the contrary, you will find that many of the topics are hard hitting especially when defending the teachings of Our Catholic Faith. Much of the subject matter is derived from my homilies along with my personal experiences and observations.

It was the recipe section that was fun. I tried to include a short commentary about the various dishes; it was a delight to sort of 'change hats' and share with you some of the things that I have enjoyed.

I hope you enjoy this book. I know I've enjoyed putting it together for you. But mostly, I hope that some time while you turn these pages, you will pause to spend a few moments in prayer because the real purpose of this book is not to entertain you, but rather, to give you food for thought.

SHEPHERD'S PIE is divided into three sections: the first, *Food for the Soul* is a collection of my articles, the second, *Food for Thought* is a collection of Ann's articles, and the third, *Food for the Body* contains some of my favorite dishes along with some hopefully interesting quips about the dishes.

It is fitting that we spend a portion of these pages on the subject of meals, because as Catholics, we have the Ultimate Meal in the Eucharist, the Perfect Food for the soul.

Bon Appetit! ...and God Bless.

Acknowledgements

Thank you to my friends, Mary Sue and Larry Eck of *Medjugorje Magazine* for permission to reprint these articles.

Thanks also to Kathleen Long, founder of the Chicago Marian Center, for permission to use my articles previously published in the Center's periodical, *Dear Children*.

This book is dedicated to all my friends who have offered me encouragement and prayerful support throughout my ministry.

Contents

food for thought...

food for the body...

Part One

Food for the Soul...

by

Father Ken Roberts

RELATING

In a Midwestern Catholic newspaper, I was recently referred to as an "ultra-conservative priest." I was really amused, especially if any of my parishioners from the late 1960's read this article. Back then I was called a "raving liberal". I seldom wore clerical clothes..in fact, I often wore a Nehru jacket with a wooden cross hanging from a leather string. I was relating. I was WITH IT!

Vatican II had just ended and I was among the first newly ordained in Rome that year. The Church was changing. The world was changing, and I was ready to change the world. I was a "new breed" priest who had all the answers. You see, I had this formula...I would relate to the kids, speak their language, be one of the guys, then I could move in and teach them about God. Seemed like a pretty good plan of action - but it didn't work.

I was successful at getting them to accept me and even like me. I was flattered that there were always young people calling and hanging around the rectory. They really took me in, even invited me to some parties, or called and asked if I would like to take in a movie. I was on a roll, or so I thought.

19

One Friday evening, the gang picked me up at the rectory and we were heading for a nearby drive-in movie. The driver of the car was a young man who had definite leadership qualities. He was personable and very likable, but somewhat of a 'big shot.' He greeted me with, "This is cool. I was grounded for some stupid thing, but when I told the old man that some of us were going to the movies with the parish priest, he said it was okay. He probably figures you're like the other priests, always trying to make us like Church, and go to confession and communion and stuff. Glad you're not like that, KEN!"

He was right. I wasn't like that. I was so busy 'relating' to their world, I had done nothing to bring them to my world and sadly, I had done nothing to bring them closer to the Lord. I had only succeeded to bring them close to me. It was strange too, because when the young man called me "Ken," I didn't feel accepted, I felt troubled. Did he respect me as a priest? Would he ever call the pastor by his first name? What had I accomplished? I was confused, but I think the kids were too.

I don't know how much the kids learned that first summer after my ordination, but I sure learned a lot about kids. Contrary to some sociologists' and educators' opinions, the kids do want rules. There's a whole world filled with temptations and trappings that pull at us. We can't tell the kids to 'let their conscience be their guide' if we have never educated them about right and wrong. I've discovered something else since those early days. It helps to let people know WHAT you are, more than WHO you are. Now, I always wear my collar when I travel because I have found that people will talk to a priest. I can't tell you how many times I have listened to the inevitable line, "I used to be an altar boy!" I have also discovered that many of the men who say that, haven't been to the Sacraments in years. I have been asked to hear confession in airports and once in an airport restaurant. The conversation that led to that would never have occurred if I hadn't been recognized as a priest from the very start.

Almost thirty years since ordination, I am still learning what it means to be a priest. I wasn't ordained to be 'one of the guys.' The most important thing I do is minister the Sacraments and the second is to teach - that includes the ten commandments.

I know the trend in many religion classes today is to stress social justice and believe me, I'm all for that, but I also feel that social justice is a natural response when we are living the Gospel. It is absolutely essential that we educate our young people and our adults, that God's laws are the fundamentals to create a better world for everyone. That is not always a popular thing to do.

Educators are facing an awesome task in today's world because the media glamorizes a hedonistic society. It's the ME, MY, I generation that acclaims, "If it feels good, do it!"

One seldom hears the word, 'sacrifice' anymore unless it pertains to a baseball game when the batter sacrifices a hit to bring a base runner home. Maybe that describes us religious educators and parents...we sometimes have to sacrifice scoring our own points for popularity to bring the runners, our kids, home.

I am overjoyed by the new Catechism, approved and recommended by the Vatican. It separates the men from the boys (and the women from the girls.) It is not speculation, it is truth. Fantastic!

You see, we priests, religious and parents are not all that different from our youth. We need guidelines too!

JUDGE NOT

Can you remember any sermon or homily that really stayed with you long after you first heard it? I can.

I just finished my second year of studies at a very strict Jesuit college in London and I was one of four students selected to study theology in Rome. It was October of 1962 and I arrived in Rome the day prior to the opening of the Second Vatican Council. My first morning in Rome I attended the inaugural Mass at St. Peter's as Pope John XXIII ushered in the Wind of the Spirit that was supposed to blow away the spiritual and theological cobwebs accumulated since the previous council. This was the old church: Latin Masses, Gregorian Chants, incense, mystery, and priests and nuns were still put on pedestals by the majority of the laity.

On the second day in Rome, we students began our retreat conducted by our vice rector. His sermon was very descriptive and spell binding. He shared an experience he had during his summer vacation when he was called to the area of Piccadilly Circus, a notorious vice spot in London where cinemas and clubs exploited sex and prostitutes were easily available. The Monsignor explained he was delayed longer than he had planned and therefore had to pass through the vice infested area after dark. It was raining hard, as it often does in England, and so he clasped the top of his raincoat concealing his Roman collar as he passed rapidly through the streets.

A drunken skid row bum, filthy and shabby, staggered along the sidewalk. His eyes were bloodshot and his teeth were yellow from tobacco. A bottle of whisky, half full, peeked out from a torn pocket of his ragged and dirty overcoat. The prostitutes who stood in the doorways pushed him from one to the other until he finally vomited and fell into the gutter. Our vice rector was about to pass by, like the priest in the Gospel, but remembering Jesus' story he, like the good Samaritan, stopped to help. As Monsignor stood over the drunken man to lift him up, his raincoat opened revealing his Roman collar. The drunk seeing his helper was a priest, whispered Latin words that shook the Monsignor to the core of his being. Words, that shook me too, back in those pre-Vatican II days when anything scandalous was hushed up so that the faithful would remain FAITHFUL. What were those words that shocked? The drunk, in his stupor, said, "Ego sum autem sacerdos." (I AM A PRIEST, TOO.)

The purpose of the sermon was to remind us that becoming a priest did not mean we would be exempt from human failings or that we could not sin or that we could not fall from grace to the gutter. The effects of that sermon, they were still called sermons then, stayed with me throughout my studies in Rome. I prayed daily for that priest and all priests who fall. Then it occurred to me in prayer, as shocking as their story was, and is, why are we not equally shocked by any Christian who falls?

Would you get drunk and then say, "Yes, I am a Christian too?" It's true that priests and sisters are Christians first with the same Jesus, the same Sacraments and commandments as you, the Christian lay person.

"Yes," you might say, "but the priest's hands are anointed, he consecrates the Host." My response is, you too are anointed in Baptism - you too receive the same consecrated Host at Mass. Wouldn't it be something if we all remembered seriously the call to holiness received by all Christians so that when we sin we could all be shocked and say, "I said that...I did that...and I'm a Christian too!"

I have recently undergone surgery and while I was in the recovery room, I realized that I could not feel my legs or move my toes. In my anxiety I imagined what it would be like to be paralyzed, unable to use my limbs. In that brief panic I concentrated on the parts of my body that were not functioning properly. I forgot that I could still see, think, breathe, and move my arms. St. Paul refers to the Church as a mystical body with parts - hands, feet, ears, and eyes. He tells us that we are all part of the body. We need all those parts to work and to be healthy and when they don't, we are handicapped. So it is with the

Church. The Church needs all of us to function properly. In the pre-Vatican II Church we concealed our sick and handicapped parts so that the faithful may remain faithful.

Today it is popular in the media to priest-bash, to reveal all the sickness in the Church and conceal the healthy body parts. Too often we hear of scandals committed by priests or religious but nothing is said about the thousands of priests and nuns who are still doing God's work. We still have Mother Teresa and one of the holiest popes of the century, John Paul II.

Yes, there are Christians who fall from grace. Yes, there are priests and religious who fall, even into the gutter, but the majority of priests, religious and laity are still striving for holiness. Let's stop concentrating on our lower limbs which seem to be paralyzed and focus more on the body that still breathes, speaks, sees and hears, then continue to pray for the parts of the body that are sick.

"We no longer look on anyone in terms of mere human judgment" (2 Cor. 5:16) We are certainly aware that the Church is human. Don't forget it is also divine!

A TRULY HOLY FATHER

Long live the Pope, his praises sound, again and yet again.

Do any of you recognize that line? It's the opening to a very popular hymn many for us grew up singing in our churches. I can't remember the last time I heard that song in the United States. Can you?

I suppose there's a reason for it but a very unsettling one. You see, it's just not a popular subject among Catholics, even clergy and religious. I can testify to that. I've experienced it many times as I go from parish to parish giving missions across the country. One thing I have learned for certain is...if I want to find out where someone stands with the Church, I only have to mention John Paul and unless he or she makes an indifferent, "Ummm," I will know immediately.

Occasionally, I hear, "He's a great Pope," But too often I hear such things as, "He's out of touch with the times," or "he's living in the dark ages," or "he needs to get with it."

Now, when they say that our pope should 'get with it', they are really saying that he should

27

bend the rules to adapt to modern society. I wonder. Modern society has glorified materialism and has become indifferent to the violence we witness each time we turn on the news.

It's my personal opinion that the reason many find it difficult to relate to the Pope is the fact that he calls us to accountability. He is the shepherd who is trying to keep his sheep from straying from the fold.

Another observation I have made about the subject of our Pope is...nobody has ever described him as not being holy. Even if they disagree with what he says, they never question his holiness. Perhaps it is that one quality in Pope John Paul that gently invites us to take another look at this man.

A good example is a story I want to share with you that happened a few years ago. I have a good friend, a nun, who is very dedicated in her ministry to retreat work and spiritual formation. The one thing we both have is a mutual respect for each other and we usually agree on most subjects. For a time she got really caught up with some modern Church thinkers who were uncertain about the Pope's stand on many subjects. She was selected to attend her Order's chapter meeting in Rome and was told before she went that she and some other members of her community were to be granted a place at Pope John Paul's private Mass and his private audience. Naturally, I was thrilled for her, but her response was "no big deal".

A few days after she returned I asked her if she was able to visit all the places she wanted to see since it was her first time in Rome. I expected her to go on and on about the Sistine Chapel, the fountains, the architecture, St. Peter's Basilica, the catacombs, all the things she said she couldn't wait to see. I asked, "What was the highlight of your trip?" To my surprise, she answered. "OUR HOLY FATHER!"

Mind you, she didn't answer, "The Pope." She referred to our pontiff as 'our holy father.' She explained how she was so moved at the private Mass because, as she put it, "I could really feel the presence of the Holy Spirit as I watched him pray...it was beautiful." She was moved by his simplicity and sincerity and she ended her account with, "we must pray for him, Ken. I think he suffers so much." I'm sure he does.

He is the shepherd leading a divided flock in a world that is saturated with materialism, in a world that constantly questions authority and in a world that is disillusioned about authority.

Our pope is continually being challenged and I'm not referring to other religions as much as other Catholics and other Church leaders. There are rumblings about schisms, about an American Catholic Church separate from Rome and we dare not speak about it for fear that we will give credibility to the movement. Subversively, those who would destroy the Church chisel away at the core of it's teachings. Their pick and hammer are doubts and confusion regarding tradition, the Real Presence, freedom of choice, false ecumenism, the papacy, and the need to relate to the people of today. We can combat the doubts and confusion through prayer and through witness. One way to begin is to pledge our allegiance to the Pope, our Shepherd.

I wish we could resurrect that old song I mentioned at the beginning of this section. I wish we could teach it to our youth as it is part of their Catholic identity. I wish we could teach our people to be proud to belong to the Church that traces it's leader back to St. Peter. I wish we would teach our kids from Scripture, (Matt.16:18) "...you are 'rock' (Peter) and on this rock I will build my Church."

LONG LIVE THE POPE!

APOLOGETICS... OR APOLOGIES

Some months ago, I released a statement from my office directing it to all the Marian Centers throughout the United States. What provoked me to do this was the deluge of mail I had been receiving over the past couple of years regarding alleged apparitions and locutions. People were asking my opinion regarding the authenticity of these claims and over and over I responded with the same answer, I DON'T KNOW!

I have enough difficulty in defending the faith without having to investigate the validity of apparitions and locutions. The thought comes to me that far too much emphasis has been focused on proving or disproving apparitions and too little energy has been spent in evangelizing the Good News.

After my first visit to Medjugorje, I was on fire with spreading the messages. Medjugorje for me was a shot in the arm. It renewed my commitment to preach faith, conversion, prayer, fasting, and peace...but these same messages are contained in the Scriptures. These messages are not new and they didn't originate at Medjugorje. Their roots are in the New Testament in the teaching of Jesus Christ.

I can see why Our Lady must keep reminding us. Just take a look at what's happening in the world, sadistic ethnic cleansing, materialism, violence, addictions to drugs, sex and power. Yes, perhaps we do need a dramatic, supernatural happening to make us stop and take notice, but let us not become so hooked on the sensational and supernatural, that we shift our gaze from the REAL miracle, the Eucharist.

I am calling attention to this because along with the large number of mail requesting information about apparitions, there is a growing number of letters directed to Church teaching and subsequent 'mixed messages' people are receiving regarding the essential teachings of our Faith. There's as much warfare going on inside the church right now as there is in Croatia. The truths of Our Catholic Faith are under attack. It is disturbing to read the letters describing the confusion regarding the teaching of the Real Presence in some parish churches and schools. More and more I find myself defending the faith among misguided Catholics. Since when has the Eucharist become a 'symbol' and not the real Body and Blood of Jesus? It's time for us to spend less time monitoring alleged apparitions and more time monitoring so called 'Catholic teaching' in our schools.

I recently spent an evening with some college students who had completed twelve or more years of Catholic education and I spent a great deal of the time defending the teaching of Eucharist. That astounds me. I'm convinced the need has never been greater than the present to incorporate apologetics in our parishes and schools. I can see defending the faith to non-Catholics, but it's disturbing to defend the faith to baptized Catholics. What's happening?

Being a Catholic is not easy in today's world. Life has become a cheap commodity and it is being snuffed out not only in Croatia, but also in the sterile surroundings of hospitals performing abortions. The pursuit of happiness has given way to the pursuit of pleasure. Amid all this contemporary confusion we have the Catholic Church saying "Come back...we have the Bread of Life!" This voice is becoming increasingly difficult to hear over the din of materialism and skepticism.

Everybody is looking for their comfort zone, and unfortunately that even has applied to teaching religion. It's uncomfortable to be questioned about the credibility of taking the Body and Blood of Jesus at Mass. It sounds too incredible. Nevertheless this IS a teaching of Our Catholic Faith and to teach this effectively we must all take a lesson taught to us by Jesus Himself. There's a parallel in the Scriptural account of the multiplication of the loaves and fishes to today's society.

In John 6: 1-15, Jesus' followers saw with their own eyes the miracle of five barley loaves and two fish feeding five thousand. But what happened later in that same chapter of John, 51-67? When Jesus told the crowd, "I myself am the

Living Bread that came down from heaven; if anyone eats this bread, he shall live forever; and the bread that I will give is my flesh for the life of the world," many found it a 'hard saying' to believe, they left Him. AND HE DIDN'T CALL THEM BACK! He didn't apologize and say, "Wait...maybe you misunderstood. What I really meant is..." Rather, he turned to his apostles and asked if they too would leave Him.

We must defend the lesson in these Scriptures. It's time to put our priorities together, to concentrate on the real miracle in the Eucharist, the second part of chapter six in John's gospel.

Just as Jesus taught truth, we must focus more on the apologetics of our Faith, but never offer apologies for what we believe.

A S K
(Always Seek the Kingdom)

A priest friend of mine tells the story of this little five year old boy who just started kindergarten. Belonging to a conscientious Catholic family, the parents were eager to show the little tot's grandparents how well he was doing with his religious instructions. It was a few weeks before Christmas; he had been enrolled now for over three months and had already learned a few prayers which had become a part of his nightly ritual. So when it was time to go to bed the grandma was invited to see how well little Johnny was doing.

Johnny knelt down beside his bed, his mom and grandma took their places across from him, and he began; "In the name of the Father, and of the Son, and of the Holy Spirit, Amen." Both parents nodded at each other proudly while Johnny recited the Hail Mary, followed by, "God bless Mommy and Daddy, my grandmas and grandpas, my baby sister, all my aunts and uncles and cousins, all my friends, and help me be a good boy." The two adults, thinking Johnny had finished, were about to close with the sign of the cross when the little guy began to shout, almost scream: "AND PLEASE, GOD, FOR CHRISTMAS, CAN I HAVE A BIKE AND SOME NEW SKATES AND..."

"You don't have to shout, son. God isn't deaf," his mother interrupted.

"But Grandma is!" Johnny replied. He wasn't taking any chances. If God didn't provide, maybe grandma would.

Johnny's story is cute, but it is also interesting to note that many of us never mature in our prayer life beyond this pattern. We begin with some devotional tools, remember to pray for those petitions entrusted to us, and then we hit God with the 'big stuff.' Give me. Get me. Grant me. Please!

Too often we go through a litany of all those things we know would make our lives better. And that's not all bad. Certainly we should ASK our Lord. It establishes confidence in His providence. Where we get into trouble is in determining our wants as opposed to our needs.

At the risk of sounding old fashioned, I still think one of the best descriptions of prayer is the definition we learned way back in the old Baltimore catechism, "Prayer is the lifting up of our minds and hearts to God." It is during this communication with our Creator that we petition Him. And Jesus taught us the perfect prayer; it's the perfect example for us to gauge our own prayer life:

"Our Father, Who art in heaven, hallowed be Thy Name. (We praise Him) Thy KINGDOM come, Thy will be done on earth as it is in heaven..."

There's that word, KINGDOM. Regardless of how many petitions we have, our first and foremost prayer should always be directed toward our eternal goal of living with God in love. "Thy kingdom come."

Notice, Jesus put it first.

The second half of the Lord's Prayer is directed toward our temporal needs, "our daily bread." This illustrates that it's okay to ask for the things we need, and it's okay to ask on others' behalf. When we promise to pray for someone's intention, aren't we saying we'll ask God to grant this favor? We could just as easily say, "I'll ask for you, too."

Asking God is easy, accepting His answer isn't always so. That's where the difference between wants and needs comes in and that's when we acknowledge that 'Father knows best,' when we submit to His plan. "Thy will be done."

Trust God. His plan is always better than ours. He will give you what you need to reach the Eternal Goal.

ALWAYS SEEK THE KINGDOM!

FATHER KNOWS BEST!

That's somewhat of an old-fashioned phrase, "Father knows best." Years ago there was even a popular sitcom by the same name. I can't tell you the last time I heard that phrase used, but it conjures up a lot of speculation. Is it because the role of the father has been watered down since so many children are being raised in single parent homes where the custodial parent is the mother? Perhaps the feminists take exception to the fact that the phrase implies that the male parent is the sole authority. Or maybe we have become so sophisticated and so emancipated that we rebel against any authority. Something to think about.

Few will argue that the ideal family consists of one mom, one dad, and children, all living in the same home working together to affirm each other with support and love. Today we know that the family unit is under much pressure, both sociologically and economically. Often it takes two salaries to support a family, so the mom isn't always as accessible as years ago. But families do survive the pressures when they work together and share the responsibilities of running a well organized home. It's a matter of priorities.

The happiest families I have visited have been the ones who worship and pray together. When God is head of the household, a certain peace prevails. Even families who have very little material advantages are rich in their relationships with one another because they pray together. During the 50's, there was a very popular slogan, "The family that prays together, stays together." No matter how corny or old-fashioned that line is...it still applies.

A few years ago, while preaching a parish mission, I accepted an invitation for dinner from a Polish family with eleven children. After the meal, the husband asked if I would like to lead the rosary. After looking down that long table at all those kids whom I assumed were anxious to do their own thing after dinner, I explained that I would be happy to lead the rosary, but I didn't want them to feel that it was mandatory or necessary to impress me.

The dad answered quickly, "Father, we have prayed the rosary together every night from the first night of our marriage through all these years. It is our family practice...your being here has nothing to do with it."

I must admit I was a little embarrassed by my suggestion, but overwhelmed by the devotion of this family, from the preschooler to the college student.

Later, the parents explained to me that having the main meal together was a priority in their home. It was where everyone gathered to share not only their dinner, but their day. Television never competed during dinner hour.

Quite the opposite of many of our contemporary families who consume their dinner while watching a TV program. Many never take a meal together because they have allowed their outside activities to take priority over family time.

Something is lost when the whole family cannot join together and share a meal. It is an excellent bonding time, not just the parent and the children, but the siblings. It's more than taking food, it's a celebration of each other!

I have said over and over in my preaching, "As Catholics, we are a family, with God, our Father...Mary, our mother, and Jesus, our Brother." And just like every family, we have rules, the ten commandments. We also have celebrations where we all come together to share a sacred meal at the Eucharist. I think young people can have a better concept of the Passover meal and the Eucharistic feast, if in their own families, family meals have been important.

There is a similar comparison with mealtime and the Mass. Just as the family comes together to be nourished and their shared meal becomes the center of their day, so the Eucharist calls us to be nourished and as Catholics, the Mass is the center of our prayer lives.

The same family that prayed the Rosary every evening after dinner, also had in a very prominent place in their dining room, a plaque that began, "God is the Head of this house." It went on to say that He was the guest at every meal. These parents were cultivating an attitude toward God and His role in their lives.

The role as God, our Father, denotes family

and it was Jesus who taught in *The Lord's Prayer* to address God as 'Our Father.'

When talking to young people, I like to direct them to think of God as a father. Unfortunately, many kids do not have a positive image of a father because their own male parent has been abusive or indifferent toward them. This is sad. So, now I ask them to think of the ideal qualities they would want in a father. God is all those things. AND HE LOVES US!

Parents, don't wait until your children go to school for them 'to get religion.' Nurture them, remind them of their real identity as children of God. Cherish them, they grow up so quickly. Forgive them, they are still learning. Enjoy them, they have a lot to offer. Love them, and never miss a chance to tell them so.

When they come to you with their problems, and sometimes the solutions aren't quite evident, when they question God's plan and you can't come up with the right answer, go to the Head of the House. Ask God to guide you. He will. And when the whole job of being a parent seems too much for you, ask God to come up with the answer. He's your Father too. AND FATHER ALWAYS KNOWS BEST!

"THERE IS YOUR MOTHER"
(John, 19:24)

I grew up with Mary... I really did! Don't say, "Mary WHO?" I'm talking about Mary, the Mother of Our Lord, Jesus. And she wasn't just a guest in our house, she was a part of the family. My own mother, Mum, saw to it.

At the end of grace at every meal, Mum would say, "Dear Blessed Mother, pray for us." Each day when we left for school, she prayed, "Dear Mother, watch over them and protect them." Finally, when she tucked us in bed at night and listened to our prayers, "Dear Mother, guard and protect them while they sleep."

Mum carried her beads in her apron pocket and all through the day, she would pray her rosary. So often, in conversation, she would say, "Well, I asked our dear Mother to..." Mum didn't say these words in a pious way, she was very matter of fact. There's no doubt in my mind that Mum habitually conversed with Mary. Our Blessed Mother was not only my mother's prayer partner, she was her work partner, her best friend and for certain her role model.

To best illustrate this, I want to share a story with you that happened right before I was to enter the seminary.

I came home late and found my mother sitting before the TV praying her rosary. That was not unusual, I often saw Mum like this. But this time she looked very worried as she listened to the report of a car accident near our home. I yelled, "Hi, I'm home!"

She answered, "Roy and Christopher were here to see you but they couldn't wait...they had to leave."

I was sorry I missed them. Roy was my big brother and Christopher, his one year old son, was my godchild. I began to ask her a question but she "Shhhed" me so I started doing something else. I heard a knock at the front door and Mum said, "Let them in, Kenny," never taking her eyes from the television. I thought she was acting very strangely since Mum was always the first to greet people when they came to call.

There at the door was our pastor, Father Walsh, and a policeman. Father merely nodded at me and went straight to my Mum. He stood beside her and took her hand, then as gently as he could, he told her that Roy and Christopher had just been killed on Bitterne Road. She had been watching the whole account on TV, but names had been withheld until relatives were contacted. Now, WE were being contacted. Words can't express the feelings that rush in when news like that is received.

I had heard enough of the news to know that one of the drivers of the two-car accident was a young teenager who was drunk, but he was uninjured. I reacted with rage. He killed my brother and nephew!

I was screaming in anger while my mother was praying in silence. She said nothing but her lips were moving and her eyes were closed. Finally, she reached for Father Walsh, who was also crying, and said, "Now I know how our dear Mother felt as she held her dead Son. We must pray to accept God's will as she did."

My mother grieved...God knows how she grieved, but she never hated or wanted revenge. In fact, she learned that this young man was an orphan and after he was found guilty at the trial, she went to him, hugged him and said she would be his 'mum'. Until she died, she sent letters, cookies and gifts to him in prison.

Where do you suppose she got all this strength, all this Christian courage? I believe it came through her intimate relationship with Jesus and His mother. You see, my mother claimed her legacy. She treasured her inheritance and really accepted Mary as her mother.

Isn't it interesting that so many Christians pass over St. John's Gospel, Chapter 19, verse 26-27? "Seeing His mother there with the disciple whom He loved Jesus said to His mother, 'Woman, there is your son.' In turn He said to the disciple, 'THERE IS YOUR MOTHER.'"

There's food for a lot of meditation in these lines. Think about it, Jesus is dying...He is in unbelievable pain and He looks down on the few at the cross who are also hurting at the sight of His suffering. Jesus is about to surrender His life, but He has one more thing to do before, 'IT IS FINISHED'. He gives us His last will and testament. "Behold your mother!"

Unfortunately, too many of us get real sophisticated as we learn more and read more. Sometimes, even our prayer life gets complicated as we search for new methods of prayer in our attempt to grow closer to Jesus, always looking for new tools to inspire us or whatever. Yet, it's all quite simple. Jesus made it that way when He referred to God as "Our Father." We are God's children. Jesus is our brother.

Jesus knew there would be times in your life when you felt alienated, when you found it difficult to pray, when you felt abandoned, misunderstood, when you couldn't stand the grief or the pain...so He gave us His mother, not only as a model, but as a real mother to turn to for comfort and support.

He gave you someone to pray WITH you and FOR you. Don't underestimate her power. Remember, Jesus worked His first miracle at her request at Cana when she, being a typical mother, was sensitive to the needs of the host and guests. Mary is sensitive to your needs too.

Claim your inheritance, BEHOLD YOUR MOTHER!

MARY HAD
A LITTLE LAMB

Don't get nervous...this is not an endorsement for Mother Goose nursery rhymes. Rather, it is simply an observation I made while visiting a family recently.

The young parents were proud that their three year old knew the Sign of the Cross. After she demonstrated it, they asked her to say her night prayers. She very obligingly went through the whole prayer, "Now I lay me down to sleep..." and she asked God to bless every member of her family, even the dog. Once again, we applauded and praised her for being such a good girl. Then, her dad pointed to a crucifix and said, "Now tell Father Ken who this is."

"That's Jesus!" She answered in a sing-song voice and proceeded to applaud for herself; again we all joined in. She was on a roll. I got carried away with the moment and asked, "Do you know about Mary?"

She nodded her head knowingly and said, "Mary had a little lamb, his fleece was white as snow..." and went through the whole nursery rhyme. We laughed and gave her the applause just the same...after all, she did know about THAT Mary!

While driving back to the rectory, I began thinking about this cute little girl and her surprise answer to my question. The strange part of this story is that the rhyme, "Mary had a little lamb," kept running through my mind like a tune you keep humming all day long. Has that ever happened to you? You hear a song and it sort of haunts you for a while?

That's what this rhyme did to me...it even interfered with my night prayers until something dawned on me, and this Mother Goose classic became a part of my meditation.

So often in Scripture, Jesus is referred to as a lamb. In John 1: 29; "when John the Baptist caught sight of Jesus coming toward him he exclaimed, 'Look! There is the LAMB of God who takes away the sins of the world.'"

In Revelations 17: 14, "...the Lamb is the Lord of lords, the King of kings..."

Even in the American Heritage Dictionary, the Paschal Lamb is defined with one word, "Christ." It was a lamb that was sacrificed by the Jewish religion in their observance of Passover; also, the lamb was the most common animal used for sacrifice throughout the Scripture. Even at every Mass, we address Jesus in the Agnus Dei, "Lamb of God, who takes away the sins of the world, have mercy on us."

Figuratively speaking, Mary had a Little Lamb. And she shared in the drama of His sacrifice from the first moment she conceived Our Lord, Jesus, until she stood at the foot of

47

the cross. Christ is our Messiah, our Savior of the world, the Chosen One who died to redeem our sins, but He was also Mary's little baby. I doubt if she thought to herself as she held His dead body at Calvary, "This is the Messiah." Not hardly, she could only mourn the cruel death of her Son which she had just witnessed.

No human being was as intimate with Jesus as was His mother. She nursed Him, changed His diapers, taught Him to feed himself, held out her arms to catch Him when He took His first steps, listened to Him say His first words, and watched Him grow from a baby to a toddler, to a teenager, to a man. She knew His favorite food, His favorite games, His best friends. She watched Him laugh and she watched Him cry. She was the first person to love Him...she was His mother.

So why do many modern religions criticize Catholics because we have so much esteem for the Mother of Jesus? It seems to me that it's just a natural response to someone God chose to be the mother of His Son.

Keep in mind, Mary has never taken any credit or called us to worship her. In Luke 1: 46, Mary quickly responds with humility and gives praise to God:

"My being proclaims the greatness of the Lord, my spirit finds joy in God my savior, for He has looked upon His servant in her lowliness; all ages to come shall call me blessed. GOD WHO IS MIGHTY HAS DONE GREAT THINGS FOR ME, HOLY IS HIS NAME."

We Catholics must never apologize for holding Mary in esteem. It is Scripturally authentic that we refer to her as "Blessed Mother." She prophesied it, "...all ages to come shall call me <u>blessed.</u>"

Through the centuries we have bestowed many lofty titles on Mary. She has been called, "Queen of Peace, Queen of Heaven, Queen of Angels, etc.." Also, many artists have portrayed her in elaborate settings, crowned with diamonds and gold, attended by cherubs. These images sometimes have a tendency to distance us. I feel the personality of Mary is best served by the paintings of the Madonna and Child, or those that depict her in a simple blue robe with her arms outstretched. She appears to be inviting us to come to her with all assurance that God loves us. That's not unlike what all mothers do with their children. We never outgrow our need for nurturing.

Mary's role was to give birth to the Son of God. At Bethlehem, she brought Jesus to us and today she brings us to Jesus. In all the recorded apparitions recognized by the Church, Mary always directs us to pray. She is our gentle Guide in our journey of faith always drawing us closer to her Son, Our Lord, Jesus.

> *Mary had a little Son,*
> *His heart was pure as snow*
> *And everywhere that Mary goes*
> *Her Son is sure to go...*

SON-BATHING
POWERFUL RAYS

The title of this article is not a typing error, it is exactly what it says, "Son-bathing," or to put it another way, Eucharistic Adoration. It's more than powerful, it's life-giving, it's nourishment for the soul, it's healing, and indeed, it's consoling. If you have any doubts, I challenge you to kneel, or sit if you prefer, before the Blessed Sacrament for one hour. I promise you will be refreshed and energized.

It's not important to arm yourself with a lot of meditative books, or a list of devotions. You may if you wish, but it really doesn't matter. What matters is that you are just 'there.' You are putting yourself in the physical presence of Our Lord, you are allowing the powerful rays of the Blessed Sacrament to touch you, to heal you, and to renew you. You are alone with your Savior, you have come to 'watch one hour with Him.' But you really don't have to DO anything...Our Lord does all the work, just be open and listen.

There's no better time to cultivate the practice of SON-bathing than during Lent, not because we are called to penance during this Holy

Season, but rather, because we are called to prayer. Did you know the word, 'lent,' is taken from the Anglo-Saxon word, 'lencten,' meaning spring? Now, when one thinks of spring, we conjure up many images, a natural flow of water, a moving forward and a season of beauty. All positive images.

I encourage you to think of Lent also in a positive way. It's time the Church has set aside for us to use for prayer and penance. Penance is to the soul what pruning is to the rosebush, getting rid of the stray branches that steal vital nourishment from the plant causing the blooms to wither before their time. During Lent we must try to prune away all those things that drain our spiritual lives. We must seek nourishment for our souls. Roses need the sun to grow...we need the SON to grow!

Most people look for things to give up during Lent. Many go back to pick up old New Year's resolutions they failed to keep, quit smoking, lose weight, and perhaps exercise more frequently. One might ask, are you pruning your body, or your soul? Lent has not been designated for physical fitness, it is for spiritual fitness...and the best gym for that is your parish church.

I urge you, spend some time during the week to come before the Blessed Sacrament. This is not a penance, it is a privilege. You have nothing to lose (or better yet, nothing to give) but a little time. If you consider how much time you spend watching television, or talking on the phone, or just wasting minutes, one hour a week hardly puts a cramp into your schedule.

Think of the many hours people spend sunbathing, getting a tan and conditioning their skin for the summer rays. They rush to the beaches, or even backyards, lay out a blanket and just lie there. Talk about wasting time! It's amusing that although we have been told over and over about the harmful rays and the damaging results of prolonged exposure to the sun, people still keep going back for more. Hours and hours are wasted getting a tan because it is supposed to make you look better.

This is especially true of my native country. Remember, "Mad dogs and Englishmen go out in the noonday sun!" Well, it's true. Not long ago, I accompanied a tour to Ireland and England; we had some very warm sunny days and the parks were filled with people. Right in the heart of London, Hyde Park was filled with sun-worshippers sprawled out on the grass. I'm certain that many used their lunch hours to catch the rays and cover their winter pallor. There they were sweating, and probably thirsty, baking in the sun. Talk about penance! And what would be their reward? Nothing more than color and in some cases, a burn.

You will never suffer any physical effect from the SON-bathing I am urging you to do. You will never suffer a burn, rather, you will experience a glow, the kind that comes from being alone with Our Lord.

Plan your schedule to include spiritual exercise, get rid of the winter pallor of the soul, spend time being a SON-worshipper. There's power and life-giving nourishment right there

before the Blessed Sacrament.
Catch the rays!

CORPUS CHRISTI

One of my favorite feasts as a child growing up in England was the feast of Corpus Christi. The feast day was always on a Thursday but we celebrated it on the following Sunday with a Blessed Sacrament procession through the streets. The sidewalks were lined with onlookers most of whom were not Catholic because the Catholics were in the procession. All the altar boys were dressed in cassocks and surplices and all the priests of the deanery were dressed in priestly vestments. Two of them accompanied the celebrant dressed in gold vestments as he carried the Blessed Sacrament under an ornate canopy. The streets were decked with banners and colorful flowers as we proudly processed from altar to altar for three Benedictions. This was the day to be 'proud to be Catholic.' It was also the day when the altar boys were treated to the movies or some other attraction. I certainly remember Corpus Christi...and even back then, we knew the meaning of the words, "Body of Christ." Now, we have a whole generation that relates to Corpus Christi only as a city in Texas.

Several years ago, I was leading a

pilgrimage to Rome and was celebrating Mass at one of the side chapels in St. Peter's Basilica. I began the Mass with just my group, but by the time we had arrived at Communion, the congregation had tripled with the many tourists who were passing by. As I gave out Holy Communion to the pilgrims I knew to be American, I said, "Body of Christ," but if the person before me appeared to be a stranger who perhaps did not speak English, I said, "Corpus Christi." I assumed that regardless the nationality or language, all would recognize the Latin, the old language of the Church.

Ten Americans approached and ten times I said, "Body of Christ," then a tall man, German or Scandanavian in appearance, stood before me. "Corpus Christi," I said as I offered the Host.

"No, Father...HOUSTON!"

He obviously had never heard of the feast of Corpus Christi nor did he understand the meaning of the words. I hoped he understood the meaning of the Eucharist and that he was receiving the true Body and Blood of Jesus under the appearance of bread and wine.

A recent survey published in the New York Times claimed that 60% of Catholics in the United States no longer believed in the Real Presence of Christ in the Eucharist. This is a shocking story if it is true because the Church has always, and still, teaches infallibly that the bread and wine at Mass, when consecrated, becomes the Body and Blood of Jesus. THIS TEACHING HAS NOT CHANGED AND NEVER WILL.

So, these Catholics who receive without

believing in the true presence should read St. Paul (1 Corinthians 11, 27-29). "He who eats and drinks without recognizing the body, eats and drinks a judgment on himself."

In the middle ages the feast of Corpus Christi was instituted by the Pope to remind the Church of the august presence of Christ in this Holy Sacrament. St. Thomas Aquinas was commissioned to write the beautiful hymn "Pange Lingua" for the occasion. Most pre-Vatican II Catholics will remember the "Tantum Ergo" verse taken from it. This was always sung at Benediction so called because we were 'blessed' with the sacred Host during the service.

I wish more parishes would take up the practice of celebrating the feast of Corpus Christi. Can you imagine the witness to others in the community if a whole parish were to gather and process with the Blessed Sacrament? Unfortunately, I have trouble even convincing some pastors of the merit of Benediction during the parish missions that I conduct.

I wish that each Catholic if they suspect the Blessed Sacrament is not held in reverence in their parish, would gather together and try to implement the practice of Benediction. It would be a good way to begin each meeting of the parish groups, the ladies' guild, St. Vincent de Paul Society, Holy Name Society and so on. It would keep the focus of the parish where it should be...on Jesus in the Eucharist. It has been my experience traveling from town to town, city to city, parish to parish, that the communities who have held this practice have kept their priorities.

The parish exists not only for a place to worship together, to minister to the needs of the people, to educate the young, to dispense the sacraments, but always to focus and hold in reverence the Blessed Sacrament.

It is the Body of Christ that keeps the Mystical Body of the Church together. It's the real reason to be *'proud to be Catholic.'*

"LORD, IF IT IS YOU"
(MATT. 14:28)

We Catholics might well ask, "Blessed Mother, is it really you...," because we are being deluged by so many claiming to have locutions. Indeed, most may be authentic because we know how much the world needs to hear the call for conversion, prayer, fasting, reconciliation and the Eucharist. With the advent of these unexplained happenings there has been interest shown by the secular media, even the entertainment media.

I was surprised when my secretary called me while I was doing a parish mission and informed me that I was invited to appear on the *Joan Rivers' Show* and talk about miracles.

"You're joking," was my response.

After she convinced me that she was not, I told her that I would have to pray about it before I made my decision. I don't mind telling you that I was nervous about it because I didn't know what to expect. One thing I did know was that Joan Rivers did not acquire her fame by talking about miracles. Yet, what helped persuade me to appear after much prayer and deliberation, was the fact that many of the people who watch the show may never get any straight answers about miracles. For the most part, they would not necessarily choose to watch anything regarding religion or the supernatural. So, armed with complete dependence on the Holy Spirit for enlightenment and courage, I accepted the invitation.

As the time grew closer for the event, I became more nervous and couldn't help but wonder if I had made the wrong decision. Suppose she made inappropriate jokes. Or what if she invited guests who were there just to dispute anything positive we could contribute about supernatural phenomena. I was filled with a lot of 'what ifs' but all my concerns and doubts were put to rest.

On the contrary, I was very impressed with the manner in which Joan approached the subject. She was very supportive and more than respectful. She even surprised all of us by producing three rosaries she had acquired from a Catholic friend and showed them to the audience. The rosaries had turned gold. I thought that took faith on Joan Rivers' part because she could very well have been criticized by many unbelievers for buying into this.

The fact that the rosaries were displayed gave me the opportunity to add that just as God could change the rosaries, so too, He can change us if we are ready to convert. Perhaps many viewers would not hear a message like that from any other source. My point is...God uses all things, people, places and situations to reach out to us. In this case, He used the Joan Rivers' Show. Our job is to be open to Him...wherever and whenever that may be.

The question that faces all of us today is,"What is real?" How do we know what is really coming from God? The question is a simple one...but the answer is not because we are saturated with messages or claims of messages from Our Lady. More and more people are coming forward claiming to have seen her or heard her. And although we know Our Lady's message is urgent, how can we be sure that all these claims are authentic? WE MUST PRAY FOR DISCERNMENT. Never before has there been such a need.

I feel certain that many claiming visions and locutions are real, but for those who are making claims for personal status or notoriety, we can only pray that Our Dear Lord and His mother will touch them and enlighten them about the seriousness of this matter.

Prayer and discernment are powerful tools...we must employ them both, then proceed with faith. When St. Peter discerned that it was really Jesus walking on the water, he went to Him. It was only when he shifted his focus away from Jesus that he became afraid and began to sink. BUT OUR LORD SAVED HIM!

He will certainly save us too. We must draw closer to Him with faith and keep focused. If Peter had not allowed the wind and the storm to distract him, his faith would not have been shaken. The wind and storm that we Catholics face today are confusion and materialism.

Friends, stay focused. Miracles are happening every day, right in your parish church. That is the one true miracle we can always count on. It's there that the simple bread and wine becomes the Body and Blood of Our Lord, Jesus Christ. Where else can we better grow in holiness and where else can our need to draw closer to Our Lord be satisfied so fully? We don't need to ask, "Lord, if it is really you..." We know it. We can feel His presence. If there is one miracle you should be open to, be open to the miracle of the Eucharist. Christ Himself, proclaimed it, THIS IS MY BODY.

If you, like many other Catholics, are trying to determine what or who is real, while praying for discernment, keep in mind that Jesus and His mother bring peace, never confusion.

PEACE BE WITH YOU.

A REASON TO BELIEVE

Faith is believing something you can't prove but 'not without reason'. We must have a reason for faith. That may not seem right at first glance but let me at least prove it to you.

How do you know there are beans in a can? Because the label says so, but that doesn't prove it. The can could have been mislabeled, right? You have proof there are beans in the can only when you open it but then it is no longer faith. There have been many floods in the last two years and many stores were flooded, enough that the cans were soaked and lost their labels. I'm sure the store owner endeavored to sell these cans but after the flood how could one tell which had beans, tomatoes, peas, or green beans? It would be blind faith for you to walk in a store and pick up an unlabeled can and say, "This is a can of beans...I believe it." No, for real faith you must have a reason to believe.

What is your reason for believing in Jesus Christ? How would you defend your faith in Him? Remember St. Thomas wanted proof - "I will never believe it without probing the nailprints in my hands, without putting my finger

in the nailmarks and my hand into His side."
(John 21: 25)

When Our Lord appeared before him and
invited him to put his fingers into the marks of
the nails, only then did he believe. "My Lord and
my God," he said kneeling in adoration.

"You became a believer because you saw
me. Blest are they who have not seen and have
believed." (John 20: 28-29)

Thomas wanted proof but once he received
proof it was no longer faith. Did he have a reason
to believe before the vision of Christ? He had
many reasons to believe, the other apostles, the
women at the tomb: all told him, "We have seen
the Lord," yet, he refused to believe. He wanted
proof.

One of the greatest reason for me to believe
in Jesus Christ is St. Paul. Have you ever tried to
change the mind of a fanatic, a bigot, a racist?
Paul, then Saul, was all of these. Only a miracle
would change the mind of the atheist, Madlyn
Murray O'Hare and cause her not only to embrace
the Catholic Faith which she hates, but to die for
it. Still, she has never helped to murder any of us
as Saul did at the stoning of St. Stephen.
Wouldn't it have taken a miracle to convert him
so deeply that he would suffer imprisonment,
torture and a painful death for Christ?

Paul said, "If Christ is not reason, we
believe in vain." As an Orthodox Ultra-
conservative Jew, would he break the first
commandment not to worship false gods and
then die preaching a false god? Would he die for
something he knew was a lie? I would find it

difficult, perhaps even impossible to die painfully for truth. Certainly not for a lie!

What if St. Paul had no vision and heard no voice? In Acts 9: 4-5, we read, "Saul, Saul, why do you persecute me?"

"Who are you, Sir?"

"I am Jesus, whom you persecute."

Do you think he would have suffered and died without that experience?

If this is not true and Paul knew he was lying, why did he die for what he knew was not truth? What about all those early Christians, most of whom were Jews, most of whom claimed to see visions or at least the witness of those who had?

Assuming that you believe in the Scriptures as Christians claim they do, would you be ready to die to defend the Word of God? And yet you are not being asked that. Rather, you are being called to be witnesses for God. Sure, it may be inconvenient at times, but how much suffering does it entail?

The analogy that I used about the can of beans was simply to illustrate that each time you visit a grocery store and buy any canned item, you are trusting the label. You are putting your confidence in the manufacturer, you are certain you are not being deceived.

Well, think about it. Would a religion that has lasted for centuries and produced thousands of martyrs not be reason to at least want to investigate that religion?

Suppose one doesn't want to go back and read and study Church history. Suppose one only wants to make a decision based on the witness of modern day Christians. What kind of witness would you be?

A non-Catholic once told me that he was vacationing with a friend and accompanied him to Mass. It seems this fellow paid attention and was quite impressed with the liturgy. Motivated by curiosity, or else as he put it, "I didn't want to be bored," he followed the liturgy with the missalette. He shared with me that he was quite impressed, but one thing bothered him. He couldn't imagine that if all this mystery that unfolded at the altar was true, why were Catholics so blase' about it.

A good point. Compare your Catholic label to the cans in a grocery. Would one know immediately that you are a Catholic Christian by your example and witness? Or are you like the unlabeled cans?

What kind of witness for the Catholic Faith are you? Would the way you practice your faith give anyone *reason to believe?*

WHEN I GROW UP

Remember way back, when a priest walked into a classroom and all the kids stood up and in a singsong voice greeted, "Good morning, Father." The priest would direct the children to be seated, then begin religious instruction. And you better believe those kids were on their best behavior because Father was there. Sister Mary was sure to get upset with them if they didn't behave and answer the questions posed to them.

Invariably, sometime during the school year, the children would be asked, "Who wants to be a priest when they grow up?" Predictably, seventy-five percent of the boys would raise their hands. (Today, you might even get a small percentage of girls if they have been exposed to the media blitz on the ordination of women.) But back then, the priest would ask, "How many of you want to be a nun?" Again, the same reaction from the girls.

I wonder how many children raise their hands today when asked that question. In fact, I wonder how often our children are even asked that question. Perhaps, not enough.

When I was in the primary grades, I used

to 'play priest.' I would set up a psuedo altar and "say" Mass. It's interesting to note that a few other seminarians who were in college with me said they did the same thing. How do you suppose Protestant kids pretend to be ministers? Maybe they set up a play pulpit and preach!

My point is that even children knew how to prioritize the duties of a priest. They connected the priesthood with Mass and they were right on target. What separates priests from all other ministers is the power to offer Mass; to change the bread and wine into the Body and Blood of Jesus. What an awesome privilege...what an awesome responsibility.

People have been generous with their description of me referring to me as a Catholic Evangelist, because, thanks to the Holy Spirit, they feel I'm a good preacher. I have more invitations than I can accept to speak at parish missions and conferences. This has become an important part of my ministry, to preach the Word, but it is NOT the most important thing I do as a priest. The most important thing I do is offer Mass. When I preach, I try to bring you to Jesus, but when I consecrate the bread and wine, I bring Jesus to you.

The Mass is the center of our prayer life as Catholic Christians. I believe it's what holds us together. It's what makes us One. But can you imagine what it would be like if nobody was there to offer Mass, if there weren't enough priests to celebrate the Eucharist?

It's a fact that the number of vocations to the priesthood and religious life has plunged in recent years. Our seminaries and convents used to be filled. Many diocesan newspapers publish a list of the newly ordained priests. It's frightening to compare the recent numbers to those twenty years ago. It's even more frightening to realize that never before have we had such a need for priesthood to be there to administer the sacraments and educate the people about the truths of Our Catholic Faith.

Today's society is saturated with all the worldly trappings. Young people set their goals to acquire material wealth, success, prestige...all the things the world promises will make their lives more comfortable, more fulfilling, and bring them happiness. Perhaps they are confusing happiness with pleasure.

When talking to young people about vocations, I always offer my personal witness. The fact that my autobiography branded me with the title, PLAYBOY TO PRIEST, I have somewhat of an advantage. Kids are curious about my background and how I earned the reputation of a playboy. I tell them the truth; there was a time as a young man when I too fell for all the worldly trappings. I wanted lots of money, lots of pleasure, lots of parties, and lots of friends who were looking for the same thing. When I finally acquired all that, I wasn't happy. Something was missing. That something was God. I was very busy pursuing my own will and I never asked what God willed. I was no longer that little boy playing priest. I ran hard and fast to deny what deep inside kept nagging at me.

When I could deny it no longer, I sought God's will and I have never for a single second regretted my 'leaving all to follow Him.' I'm sharing this with you because maybe one of you reading this article is experiencing similar feelings. Maybe something is missing in your life. Maybe you feel you're supposed to be doing something more. Ask God what He wants for you.

As I said in the beginning of this section, the class was asked, "Who wants to be a priest?" That was a question directed toward little children. When I talk to young men today, I ask, "Who feels they are being called to the priesthood?" I tell them I felt the call before I felt the desire.

Even now, when I get bogged down with pressure, God sort of nudges me and I get things in the proper order. Just recently, while conducting a parish mission, I decided to take a walk and work out some of the nervous energy. I was up tight because my schedule was loaded with missions, conferences and retreats. I knew there was a mound of mail waiting at the rectory when I returned home, not to mention the appointments I had to keep. I felt anxious and worried.

As I was circling the empty schoolyard, the bell rang for recess and it seemed like a stampede of children poured out of every door in the school building. I stood there watching them at play for a few minutes and thought I was pretty much unnoticed until I felt a tug at my sleeve. When I looked down there was this little boy, about six or seven, staring at me. He asked simply, "Do you like bein' a priest?"

I'm seldom at a loss for words, but this little

guy took me off guard. His question made me sift through all that was running through my mind and redirect my thoughts.

"Yes, I like being a priest," I answered. He obviously didn't want to hang around while I elaborated because he simply replied, "Oh," and ran off to join his friends. I don't know what was going on in that little fellow's mind, or what provoked him to ask me that question, but I'll always be grateful that he did. It put things in the proper perspective.

I pray I'll never take my priesthood for granted; that I'll always be mindful of the most important thing that I do...offer Mass and minister the Sacraments. I wish somehow I could express to young men thinking about a vocation, how much the priesthood has meant to me. I thank God for allowing me to be a part of His Church in this special way.

I think it is appropriate for me to insert at this point, a dedication I wrote in one of my books:

To the many thousands of wonderful men, some of whom I know...most of whom I don't...many of whom are extrordinary...most of whom are not. They are black, white, red, yellow, tan. They are in every field of endeavor, on every corner of the earth. They are saints and sinners, the greatest international brotherhood the world has ever known...my brother priests. God bless them!

WHOSE SINS YOU
SHALL FORGIVE

Unless you live in a jar, you must be aware of the negative publicity clergy have been receiving lately. I'm not referring to just newspapers or magazines, I'm talking about daytime controversial talk shows. Rather than give them notoriety in this article, I will not mention their names...but you know who I mean.

The producers know that they will draw an audience at the opening of the show if they mention the nature of the scandal, and emphasize the transgressors as "Father X, or Sister X, or Brother X." This especially applies to sex scandals. Immediately telephone terminals throughout the nation light up as the viewer rushes to the phone to tell a friend or relative to tune in. This is juicy stuff and it generates a tremendous response from the viewing public. After all these people are supposed to be celibate!

For many who are critical of the Church these shows provide them with ammunition. They make remarks, "The Church is going to have do something...it's not NORMAL for people to never have sex!"

Or maybe you've heard this one, "They better start letting priests and religious marry because the church is going to be loaded with a bunch of perverts!"

Then we hear from our fundamentalist brethren, "The Bible in Genesis 2, verse 18, says, 'it is not good for man to be alone.'"

When I'm called upon to respond to the above Scripture, I refer to Matthew 19: 11-12, regarding celibacy. Jesus said, "Not everyone can accept this teaching, only those to whom it is given to do so. Some men are incapable of sexual activity from birth; some have been deliberately made so; AND SOME THERE ARE WHO HAVE FREELY RENOUNCED SEX FOR THE SAKE OF GOD'S REIGN. LET HIM ACCEPT THIS TEACHING WHO CAN."

I could present pages in defense of the Church's teaching regarding celibacy because I support the Holy Father's stand. But what I really want to address in this article is the confusion created by some of our 'stray' clergy and religious. Aside from being hot copy and juicy topics for talk shows, something else has resulted. WE ARE ALL SUSPECT...and I resent that.

I'm not going to deny that priests never sin, and I'm not going to deal with that. That's Our Lord's job. What I do have to deal with as a priest is the hurt it brings to the people and the damage it does to the faith of the people of God.

I remember some years ago at a social gathering, a woman approached me with this statement, "I used to be a Catholic, but this priest I knew insulted me. Now, I don't want anything to do with the Church!" She was vehement about her resentment toward the whole Church, so I asked her, "Do you mean you left the Church because of one priest?"

"Yes!" she answered emphatically.

After a quick prayer to the Holy Spirit, I answered, "I am very sorry for your pain and on behalf of Holy Mother Church, I apologize and beg your forgiveness."

She was dumbfounded but I explained that if she could blame the whole Church because of one priest, perhaps she could accept the apology of one priest on behalf of the whole Church.

We all know that many people look for reasons to alienate themselves from the Church. It's not easy to be a Catholic. If someone is looking for weaknesses, he or she is certain to find them because of one fact; the Body of the Church: the hierarchy, the clergy, the religious, and the laity, is made up of people. People sin! Holy Orders and vows made by religious and married folks do not insulate us from sin. We still have our humanness, our weaknesses, our virtues and our faults.

That is why it is so vital that each of us has a prayer life. The sacraments and prayer are the only tools we have to fight the temptations of the devil. And believe me, some of the stories that we, the public, have been exposed to through the media are diabolical because they result in people doubting their faith; not to mention how they begin to doubt the priests and religious. One priest has an affair, so that must mean that all priests mess around.

You know, we can't get media coverage of the priests who are working, praying, sacrificing, serving unselfishly, remaining pure, and bringing people closer to God. These guys aren't controversial and they don't draw an audience.

Our poor laity has been burdened with so many statistics and polls that it is no wonder they are confused. They read about the percentage of priests who are gay, or who have had affairs. Where do they come up with these figures? I have been a priest for almost thirty years and I have yet to meet one priest who has been approached by the almighty poll.

Dear friends, pray for us. We need your support because we are taking a beating. I'm not denying that some priests have fallen and created scandal, and I'm not defending them, nor am I asking you to forgive the sin. But I am asking you to forgive the sinner...Christ did. We can derive something good from these exposes, if it urges us to realize the need for prayerful support. Set aside a minute each day to pray for us that we may be worthy of your trust. Pray that we may serve you and bring you closer to Our Divine Savior. Pray that we may live up to your expectations. Pray for all of us to be aware of what we are and what God expects us to be.

For all the priests who have fallen, pray for them too. Remember we're just like you; we're trying to get to heaven in spite of our weaknesses. Pray for compassion for your priests...*whose sins you shall forgive.*

I DID IT ALL
FOR YOU

So often, we clergy or others in ministry go to Medjugorje to do for others. This was one of the times I was ministered to in Medjugorje.

It happened in August of 1990, I had a double group of teenagers; 120 of them with the first pilgrimage followed by 135 on the second, with one day's break in between.

I had stopped smoking a year before, but started again. When a non-smoker starts smoking again, we smoke twice as much as we ever did. I was more addicted than ever in my life, and I've smoked since I was thirteen (not proud of it). However, I've always stopped during Lent, except for Sundays which never counted. It was a good mortification, though I always cheated. Even when I stopped smoking, I always cheated. I did make certain that I removed the temptation, by not having cigarettes around. A close friend shared an observation about me and my Lenten practice regarding cigarettes. "I figured it out, Father Ken, you don't give up smoking for Lent, you give up buying cigarettes."

Smokers will tell you that when they are

under stress, they smoke more. That's how it was with me. I was up to a pack and a half per day, especially in Medjugorje. I'd celebrate Mass, light a cigarette; give a talk, light a cigarette; have a meal, light a cigarette; stop for coffee, light a cigarette; if someone stopped to talk, light a cigarette; take a minute out to relax, light a cigarette.

The teens came to me and said, "Father, we're really worried about you. You're smoking too much. We don't like your smoking at all." One of them even said, "Don't you believe your body's a temple of the Holy Spirit?"

"Yes," I answered.

"You keep telling us our bodies are temples of the Holy Spirit, right?" he asked. There were a whole bunch of kids sitting there listening to this: I almost felt as if they were ganging up on me.

"Right," I answered again.

"Father, don't you believe what you preach?"

"Yes, I do."

"Father, if you really believe that your body is a temple of the Holy Spirit, why do you smoke?"

"Because I'm incensing it!" I got a laugh from the kids, except for one little girl who had tears in her eyes. A strange reaction, I thought.

They bugged me and bugged me and bugged me the whole week. And the more they bugged, the more I smoked. "Don't be so righteous. There are more important things to worry about." I tried desperately to get them off the subject.

I hope this story helps others with

addictions. There are all kinds; addictions to food,
alcohol, power, sex, and fame. Anything that
controls our lives that we rationalize about...that
we're not in charge of, is an addiction.

I was certainly addicted to cigarettes. I
figured I could've been addicted to worse things,
but it was still an addiction. I didn't control
cigarettes; they controlled me. As soon as I left
the pulpit, as soon as I climbed up Mt. Krizevac, or
Apparition Hill, I'd light up. I even smoked
making the Stations of the Cross on the way up
the mountain, saying I needed a rest, but what I
really wanted was a smoke.

No wonder the kids were worried!

The last night there, on the vigil of the
Assumption, the kids were sneaking out of the
house at midnight; about twenty of them. I heard
this noise going on and I was suspicious they
might be going to the bar. They had their shoes
off. They were tiptoeing out of the house.

I asked, "Where are you all going?"

"We're going to climb Mt Krizevac."

"It's midnight!" I said.

"We know...we're going to spend the night
up there in prayer."

"You are going to spend the night on the
mountain in prayer? Why?" I was suspicious.

"It's for you, Father."

"For me?"

"Yes, so you'll stop smoking!"

So I said, "Well that's very nice of you,
but why aren't you wearing shoes?"

"We're doing it for you."

I was moved, but it didn't stop me from

smoking. I thought I better smoke more that night because I'd feel too guilty smoking in front of them tomorrow.

The next morning, after they came back, one of the girls was having difficulty getting her shoes on. Her feet were all bruised and cut from the rocks. I said, "You know, you really should have worn your shoes."

"I know, Father," she said, "but I did it for you."

She lifted up her bloody foot and said, "See my bloody foot?"

"Yes."

"Every time you get an urge to smoke, remember that my feet are bleeding for you."

The kid started to cry...and so did I. Later, I thought, "Jesus, YOU did that for me."

So I'm telling all of you who read this article, whatever your addiction or your sin is...His Feet bled for you, so did His Hands, so did His Back, so did His Side, so did His Head. Every part of Him bled for you. Christ climbed a mountain for us, and He died there before the morning came.

Perhaps it will help you, as it did me, to keep that in mind during times of temptation. I must admit, I rationalized the incident away several times over the past five years when I went back to the habit, but I always quit again until now, I am no longer addicted to cigarettes.

To all my teen friends who made the sacrifice for me...it paid off. Thank you!

CONVERSION CRASH

Many stories of conversion have come from Medjugorje and I know I have related a good number of them. I have personally witnessed conversions on each trip I have taken, and to give an account of all would fill this whole book, so I decided to share with you something else I have witnessed. I call it, "conversion crash." It seems to occur after the travelers return to their homes and their daily routine, and it is manifested in the form of confusion and sometimes disappointment.

In Medjugorje, people witness to each other. I have never spoken to one pilgrim who has not mentioned how moved he or she was by the reverence of the people, not only the people who live in the village, but also the other visitors. Most people speak about how inspirational the liturgies are and how impressed they are by the number of people lined up for confession, and that includes thousands of young people. They say the Mass comes alive and has more meaning for them. They talk about how they have learned to really meditate on the mysteries of the rosary. And they all come away with a greater reverence for the Eucharist. Too often, when they return home and resume their daily lives, they believe the peace they experienced in Medjugorje is being threatened by skepticism and criticism, not only by family and friends who have not been to Medjugorje, but also by the clergy and religious.

The confusion sets in because one can't help but wonder why a priest or religious would not endorse anything that focuses on prayer and enhances the practice of daily Mass. And the disappointment sets in because it is only natural to want to share with others, especially other Catholic Christians, a religious experience that has changed our lives.

I'm certain that is why so many people return to Medjugorje and why the Marian Centers and Medjugorje Conferences have been so successful in getting large numbers of people who want to gather together...it's almost like a "support group." There's comfort in knowing that others share your views, your experience, and your desire to "spread the word."

I've heard the Medjugorje movement referred to as a cult, and in light of the negative connotation of that word, I take exception. We are accused of being extreme in our devotion, but what are we devoted to? Prayer, conversion, fasting, the Eucharist, the rosary, hardly subversive activities!

But there IS subversive activity and it's going on right before our eyes. When Father Pavich appeared on Mother Angelica's program, he spoke about the attack the Church was undergoing in America. He said that Medjugorje was under fire by artillery we could see and hear, but the artillery being used against our Church was not so visible. The very truths of our faith are being attacked from within.

Many Catholic churches have removed all images of Our Lady and they have placed the Blessed Sacrament in some obscure place where it's difficult to recognize if the church is Catholic! In some cases, the crucifix has been replaced with some abstract art that one has difficulty identifying, or sometimes there's a banner with some catchy phrase designed to boost spiritual awareness...whatever that's supposed to mean.

Many people have told me that their Sunday homilies concentrate on social justice and that's okay, but I maintain that social justice is a natural response when we live the Gospel... so, why not just preach the gospel? Our Lord gave the perfect formula for social justice in Matthew 22: 39, "Love your neighbor as yourself."

The people who are most critical of the Medjugorje movement are often the same people who use these phrases: spiritual consciousness, wholeness, global awareness, religious liberty, agenda, social change, and planetary consciousness. Impressive, but confusing.

I agree with Father Pavich about the Church being attacked, but I also believe that it can be saved by the majority of our people who want to preserve our truths and traditions. And I believe that we Catholics who have experienced Medjugorje can be an important part of that process. We know what we have witnessed in that little village. We've seen people join together and worship Our Lord and Savior at Mass. We've seen people change their lives and live the gospel. We've seen the joy and we've experienced the peace.

On the last Medjugorje trip I made, at the airport as we were preparing to return home, one lady said to me, "I wish I could bring my whole family and all my friends here so they could see what the Church can be." Well, that may be impossible, but we can bring Medjugorje home with us, not geographically, but spiritually.

Don't fall victim to 'conversion crash' by allowing the confusion and disappointment to get to you. Never take the peace and joy you experience in Medjugorje for granted. Nurture it with continued prayer and daily Mass when at all possible. You can be instrumental in preserving our Catholic Faith and protecting it from those who would destroy it. You can be couriers of the message of Our Blessed Mother by your witness.

Today, when we hear so much about New Age, let us join together with New Commitment. "They will know we are Christians (and that we have been to Medjugorje) by our love!

"SUFFER THE LITTLE CHILDREN.."
(MATT: 10:14)

"War is hell!" That's more than a quote, it's a fact. One only needs to turn on the news broadcasts and see the human suffering caused by war. When you hear the fatality stats, when you hear the numbers, keep in mind that each number was someone's husband or wife, father or mother, sister or brother. The body count never measures the tears.

We can't help but wonder if any cause can be worth so much human suffering, especially to the children. Recently, I watched a television program which focused on the children in the former Yugoslavia. I saw children who were crippled, blinded, paralyzed, and burned from bullets and bombs. Many of them have lost one or both parents so if they are fortunate enough to recover, they may well be orphans. The physical scars they bear will never be as devastating as the emotional scars that will influence their attitudes toward the world around them. These are the Holy Innocents of today; the victims of a war most of them are too young to understand, but old enough never to forget.

When the cameras panned the filled wards, the viewer couldn't identify Serbian children, Muslim children, or Croatian children...they are suffering children whose destinies are determined by the results of war. This scene conjures up many feelings in all of us and always the question, WHY?

Probably the most difficult thing for me, and for many other clergy, is to offer an appropriate answer to that question. Too often, we are asked, "Why does God allow this to happen?" But God doesn't create the war, man does. We have the will to choose good or evil and the responsibility to accept the consequences of our choice. Killing, suffering, fighting never stem from what is good...that can only be evil. How can anyone deny the existence of the devil when looking at a war? Power and greed are the tools he uses to entice people to inflict such pain on each other.

So, what can WE do? There's a connotation of frustration when the question is posed that way. Better to ask, WHAT can we do? It's obvious that we cannot take up arms and join in the fighting, or assume an Indiana Jones persona and lead the good guys against the bad guys. WHAT we can do, begins with each of us individually and personally. It's not easy and will require some sacrifice (a word not often used in our modern society), but it is what we CAN do.

We can live the message of Medjugorje given to us by Our Blessed Mother. It's not a coincidence that the Queen of Peace chose to appear in a country that is now torn apart by war. When Our Lady first began appearing, the fighting had not yet begun and I'm certain that most people had no idea of the urgency of the messages, but now, time has demonstrated the acute need to take the messages to heart, then LIVE them.

The frustration that wells up when watching accounts of the victims of the war will not be as crippling if each of us knows in our heart that we are doing what we can to help the suffering. By our contributions to the Croatian Relief and living the messages, we are doing WHAT WE CAN DO!

Unfortunately Bosnia is not the only place where we find suffering among the children. This is a worldwide circumstance that haunts all of us. Little kids are robbed of their childhood fantasies and forced to face the cruel reality of starvation and pain. They are victims of an older generation's vengeance. Too often the children are taught, "an eye for an eye," rather than, "Love thy neighbor as thyself." The results are what we witness on the newscasts today, whether it be across the ocean or in our own neighborhoods. Groups of unhappy kids can become gangs of angry teenagers. This has become one of the biggest problems facing law enforcement in the United States today. Have we forgotten how to nurture and protect our children? Has the quest for power, money, territory, taken priority over the welfare of children? God help us!

The title of this section is taken from Matthew 10: 14. If you turn to the more modern translations of the Bible, you will read, "let the children come to me," but I prefer to use the old translation, "SUFFER the little children," because I think it more appropriately describes the children of Bosnia-Herzegovina. We can only pray that these children will survive this war with hope and love and not fall victim to the evils of hate and revenge. That's why our prayers and living the Medjugorje message is so vital...it's for the children. Who can turn away from a child in need?

There are many, many children who will not survive this war, but we can offer consolation by referring to that same Scripture passage. "Let the children come to me; do not prevent them, for the kingdom of God belongs to such as these."

CHOICES

I'M PRO-CHOICE!...and I choose life!

That's how I respond to the issue of abortion when the subject comes up in an interview because frankly, I'm sick of listening to this issue being sugar-coated and disguised as women's rights, or civil rights. And I'm one hundred percent certain the public opinion would be swayed if our so-called pro-choice people would say it like it is, if they carried their banners with the real message, "I'M PRO-MURDER!" After all, that is the result of their cause.

I won't disguise the opposition with the title of Pro-choice in this article. I'll refer to them as Pro-abortion: I won't be a part of the deception.

The pro-abortion activists have tried to convince the American public that women are being robbed of their civil rights if they are not able to terminate a pregnancy. They pose such arguments as pregnancies resulting from rape, but I'd like to know how many abortions were performed last year on rape victims, as compared to the overall numbers of abortions performed. The statistics are so minimal they wouldn't be worth quoting to support their argument. I'm opposed to abortion as a result of rape too...there are many adoption facilities to handle what society calls, 'unwanted pregnancies'...when the commodity that really is being dealt with is unwanted children. Still, there are thousands of couples praying to adopt a child. Unwanted pregnancies can produce WANTED CHILDREN.

So what about the argument that women have the right to choose if they want a child or not? I agree that women do have that right, but make the choice before the pregnancy occurs.

CHOOSE abstinence during appropriate monthly cycles. CHOOSE chastity on a date. CHOOSE self-control if it's not the right time to accept the responsibility of a child. CHOOSE to control your own destiny. CHOOSE to take control of your life. CHOOSE not to be deceived by abortionists. CHOOSE to look at the real issues.

Pro-abortion people like to say women are victimized...but they're wrong. The real victims of the abortion issue are the babies, the millions of babies who have been slaughtered for the sake of convenience.

Another tool the pro-abortion groups like to use is confusion, and they'll find a few medical so-called 'experts' who will argue about when life begins in the womb. To me, this is one of the most absurd arguments of all.

Once I was a guest on a radio talk show when the abortion issue came up and a caller asked me to prove when life begins in the womb. I answered that I don't have to, since I'm not the one who wants to kill it! But I also ask people to refer to any medical text that shows the development of the unborn child. There's LIFE in that embryo. There's LIFE in that fetus. What kind of life? HUMAN LIFE, a baby.

This whole issue is frightening. Has our society become so hedonistic that life has become such a cheap commodity? Has convenience become a greater goal than morality? Can politicians strive to end child abuse while they fight to legalize abortion? ABORTION IS THE ULTIMATE CHILD ABUSE!

So what are we going to do about it?

Many things. We can educate ourselves about the people we choose to represent us in the legislature. We can support the Pro-Life groups' endeavors. We can educate our young people about morality. We can march. We can demonstrate.

But be cautious about WHAT you demonstrate. Some recent demonstrations have proven to be unsuccessful and confusing, even causing pain to many innocent parties. Demonstrations should only be coupled with sensitivity. I don't see any positive purpose being served by a few of the pro-life demonstrators who shout and scream their beliefs. I think the most effective demonstrations are the ones that demonstrate prayer and call upon God to take control. I can't think of any witness we can give that is more powerful than a group gathered together to pray for the unborn children.

And folks, pray for the mother who has chosen to terminate her baby's life. Perhaps she was raised in an environment that told her abortion was okay, that it was a moral solution to an unwanted pregnancy. Maybe the simple truth is that she just doesn't know any better.

The fact may be hard for you and me to accept but it is a fact. We have a whole generation out there who has been brought up with, "if it feels good, do it." It's the ME, MY, I society that has made victims of not only the unborn babies, but all of our youth.

We Catholics are blessed to have a beautiful prayer, taken directly from Scripture, the "Hail Mary." And I would ask all of you to think about the prayer with me now.

"Hail Mary, full of grace, the Lord is with You: most blessed are you among women and blessed is the FRUIT OF YOUR WOMB." (Luke 1: 42)

Blessed is the fruit of EVERY womb that carries an unborn child because God has breathed life into it. The greatest demonstration we can all join is prayer. Saying the HAIL MARY, the repeated recitation of that prayer in the Rosary, is a constant reminder of the 'fruit of every womb.' IT'S PRO-LIFE!

WINGS OF FAITH
THE LUTHERAN WHO TEACHES CATHOLICS

A highlight for me recently in witnessing to Our Lady and the power of the rosary was meeting a young Lutheran man named Richard.

I was preaching a diocesan Catholic retreat in Erie, Pennsylvania at the seminary. It was by reservation only because they could hold just 200 a day. They had me give the retreat to two different groups.

The first day there was this young man sitting on the aisle in a wheelchair. My eyes were drawn to him. He was completely paralyzed from the neck down. He couldn't even move his fingers. He had braces on his hands and around one hand a rosary was wrapped. He sat there with the most beautiful smile on his face. There was such radiance that it appeared he was lit up.

I've never seen a happier face. He was a handsome young man about 21 years old. During the break he put this tube in his mouth - it was like a microphone tube - and I guess he blows in it. Whatever he does, it propels the wheelchair. He can also steer it, somehow moving his head.

He propelled himself over to me and said, "I'm so excited about seeing you, Father, I watch you on EWTN."

He said he'd come all the way from the Cleveland, Ohio area, a long drive from Erie. His mother had brought him in one of those special vans that carry wheelchair platforms. I was intrigued by his story, especially when I learned he was Lutheran.

Richard was hit by a drunken driver when he was sixteen and left completely paralyzed. There was no bitterness in him as he told his story, no depression. He was so elated, so excited, so vivacious. It was incredible.

At that time I'd just had an impacted tooth extracted, after already having an infection plus surgery on my gums. This had been going on for three months and I was feeling depressed. I had a constant drainage in my mouth and it hurt to talk. So here I was worried about sore gums and an extracted wisdom tooth, trying to keep my spirits up and getting mad at God, wondering when He was going to heal me. Now this young man comes along who can't even move his little finger. It's not been three months for him but five years and he'll never heal.

When I asked him, "Aren't you bitter toward the boy who hit you?" he said, "No, I've forgiven him because Jesus says we have to forgive."

"Well," I said, "aren't you bitter toward God?"

"No, if this thing hadn't happened to me I wouldn't have known Jesus. I can't do anything else, so what I do all day long is watch EWTN - I love your programs. And when I'm not watching television I pray the rosary."

I looked at his hand. "Can you move that rosary?"

"Oh no," he told me. "My mother puts it between my fingers. Sometimes I lose count count and say fifteen Hail Marys instead of ten for a decade. If I'm not sure I've said ten, I say extra ones."

"You keep praying the Rosary?"

"Yes, I pray for the holy souls in Purgatory."

"But I thought you were Lutheran."

"I am," he said, "but I'm really Catholic in my beliefs. I watch EWTN, I've watched all your programs, I've read your books."

"How can you read my books?"

"I have this special attachment to hold the book and I turn the pages with my tongue."

By this time, I'm in tears. This boy is so radiant! I wish all of you readers could see his face. I'm repeating myself, I know, but I've never seen a more joy-filled face. Imagine the greatest love story you've ever seen - the face of someone in love - how it radiates. Richard's face was like that only a thousand percent more. It was so outstanding that everyone in the church noticed it.

I asked him if he'd ever thought about becoming a Catholic. He said he wanted to be Catholic. He told me one thing he missed was not receiving Jesus in the Eucharist.

"Why doesn't your minister bring it to you?"

"He could, but it's not the real thing. He's not a priest," he answered.

"You know a lot about Catholics."

"Oh," he said, "I know more about being a Catholic than most Catholics. My Catholic friends come to me to find out about their faith."

"Where did you learn so much?" I asked.

"There's this nun friend who comes over. She taught me to pray the rosary and she prays with me."

When I heard there was a nun involved in his spiritual life, and that he knew about the Catholic Faith, I felt encouraged to see about accepting him into the faith without having him go through the whole RCIA program. It would've been difficult for him with his handicap.

The pastor was there, and with his approval, I could have registered Richard and received him into the Church.

I said to him, "How would you like to become Catholic right away?"

He said he'd pray about it. This showed his maturity. He discussed it with his mother and she had no objections. But Richard was afraid his becoming Catholic so suddenly might hurt his father, who was a devout Lutheran.

"I have to pray more about it," he concluded. "I don't want to just surprise my father with it. I want to prepare him first.

We left it at that. However, during Mass I had everyone offer their Communion for him.

Later he came up to witness while I held the microphone. He told the congregation how lucky they were to be Catholic, how great it was that they had known the Blessed Mother since their childhood; he had only recently discovered his Mother, Mary. He talked about the power of the rosary and told everyone to pray the rosary and stay close to Mary's Immaculate Heart and to the Sacred Heart of Jesus.

This young Lutheran had all the Catholic adults and teenagers in tears. I told him, "I'm going to preach about you wherever I go."

He just smiled, nodded and said, "Praise Jesus."

In a world where the majority has become spiritually paralyzed, this young man soars on wings of faith and joy. He may be physically handicapped, but spiritually, he's one of the healthiest souls I have had the pleasure... no, the gift, to meet.

God bless you, Richard.

"THE DEVIL MADE ME DO IT!"

Some of you may remember a popular comedian named Flip Wilson. He had a weekly variety show on television and one of the many characters he portrayed was a preacher called, "The Rev," from the church of "What's Happening Now?" It was a satire on some modern day evangelists who live more by the philosophy of, "do as I say...not as I do." Well, 'The Rev' had a way of excusing himself of any transgressions by comically explaining, "the devil made me do it!" I must admit he was quite entertaining and indeed his whole act was to poke fun at ourselves, but there was something quite profound in his subtle message. Most of us don't want to admit our wrong doings; it's always easier to blame someone, or something, else. In this case the preacher blamed the devil.

The mere fact that the devil was part of a comedy act, enforces this truth; most people don't take the devil too seriously. And even as I write this article, I am convinced that this is a very unpopular subject. Many people don't believe that the Evil One exists, while others find the subject of the devil toounpleasant to address. As a result, in the past few decades, Satan has been shelved. Preachers quit preaching about him and educators quit educating about him. It's almost as if modern society has been in a state of denial.

It was the entertainment media that resurrected the subject of the devil. Remember the book, and subsequent movie, "The Exorcist"? It was truly a horror film, and most importantly to the movie industry, it made money. Though horrifying, it wasn't taken too seriously. Rather, it was put in the same category of other bizarre films designed to 'scare the hell' out of you. Many movie makers hopped on the bandwagon and made money by producing more 'devil' pictures. The devil made for good box office!

Before William Peter Blatty wrote THE EXORCIST, he had acquired a reputation as a fine playwright. Having been educated by the Jesuits, Blatty had heard of the story about a St. Louis Jesuit, Father William Bowdern, who had performed a successful exorcism. He researched the story as well as similar stories that had been documented and came up with the book, then later, the movie. Fr. Bowdern was a very holy man: his experience at the real exorcism were as dramatic as the movie. Be assured, this dedicated priest would be the first one to proclaim that the devil does exist.

When taken out of the realm of theater, Satan is an unpopular subject and quite frankly, I hesitated to even write this piece. Yet, while we've been so busy avoiding talking about Satan, there is evidence that his power and his following are growing all the time. Never before have so many satanic cults existed, and part of the purpose of these cults is not only to worship Satan, but to bring suffering and death to people. Human sacrifice is a part of the ritual. Many law officers believe that the great number of missing children is a result of the cults' rituals. That fact is more terrifying to me than any movie produced in Hollywood.

It is also reported that Our Lady has warned us repeatedly about the diabolical influence in today's world, including the destruction of natural resources. Look what happened in the Persian Gulf. The oil spills will take years to clean up and there's still no way to measure the extensive damage it will do to marine life. What about the burning oil wells in Kuwait? Ecologist and scientists maintain that the vast amounts of smoke released into the atmosphere will hinder vegetation in that region, and they are still anticipating just how far reaching the damage will be.

So what can we do about it? We expose Satan...we admit he exists. By denying him, we give him room to move freely. Then, we keep our eyes fixed on God, Who has dominion over him. We stay faithful to the Holy Eucharist and we pray for discernment to know what is truly of God. Evil is often disguised as good, but when we follow God's plan, we'll always have peace. Just a couple of years ago, people all over the world fought a war right in their own living rooms before the television sets. We prayed for our leaders and the young men and women on the battlefields. We raised our flags, displayed yellow ribbons and in some churches, sang patriotic songs. Our chests swelled with emotion at sports and entertainment events when we sang the National Anthem. After some masses, we sang, GOD BLESS AMERICA, and it took on new meaning because we were at war. We were involved!

Friends, we're still at war, but too often we don't recognize our enemy. There's a battleground of good vs. evil, truth vs. deception, pro-life vs. pro-choice, values vs. pornography, wellness vs. drugs. Every day we choose which side we'll take in this battle. We must be vigilant and mindful that the devil does exist, though we don't always recognize him.

We have the most effective artillery available; Mass, the Eucharist, and the rosary. Prayer and sacrifice are important parts of our training. Peace and Eternal Life are our rewards.

Perhaps some of you remember back when we recited prayers at the foot of the altar after Mass. We said three Hail Marys, Hail Holy Queen, a few aspirations, and a prayer that is still very appropriate for today's world; the Prayer to St. Michael. He's our five star general, whose purpose is to protect the people of God. Make it part of your daily prayers.

St. Michael, the Archangel, defend us in battle. Be our protection against the wickedness and snares of the devil. May God rebuke him, we humbly pray, and do you, Oh Prince of the Heavenly Hosts, by the power of God, cast into hell, Satan and all the evil spirits who prowl about the world seeking the ruin of souls. Amen.

DON'T GIVE UP, JUST GIVE!
(Lent)

Most of us approach the new year with loads of resolutions..and, if we fail, we get another chance to start all over during Lent. "I'm giving up candy for Lent," or maybe it's, "I'm giving up desserts," or "I'm giving up eating between meals," or "I'm giving up smoking." All the above mentioned are great sacrifices, but what we need to ask ourselves, and answer honestly is; *are we motivated by spiritual fitness or physical fitness?*

Are we concentrating on what we are giving up to be physically healthy and look better or what we can give ourselves to be spiritually healthy? That includes giving ourselves more time for prayer and reflection.

It's true that Lent is considered a penitential season; it's that time in the liturgical year when we take an inventory of our spiritual fitness and prepare ourselves for Easter Sunday. We are called to make sacrifices through fasting, special prayers and almsgiving. The Church has long recognized these tools as 'Nautilus equipment' for the soul and in her wisdom, has given us all

we need to shape up spiritually during this time
of the year.

Recently I had a physical and was told that I
need more exercise. It seems the only real exercise
I get, is walking through the terminal in airports.
Until now, I have used the excuse that I just don't
have the time...I have more important things to
do. Now, faced with high blood pressure, high
cholesterol and a high reading on the scale, I'm
faced with my moment of truth. I can't use the
old excuses anymore and it's imperative that I
make the time to do what is necessary to be
healthy again. I was reminded that our bodies are
temples of the Holy Spirit, so we have an
obligation to pursue good health and take care of
the bodies entrusted to us. It's sort of a case of,
Physician, heal thyself!

Just as I have made excuses why I can't do
physical exercise, many of us find excuses why we
can't do spiritual exercise. Does this sound
familiar? "It's so hard to get to Mass every day...I
have such a heavy schedule," or, "The Church
just isn't the same as it was years ago," or even,
"Well, since they let women give out
Communion, I stay away." I have even heard, "I
don't have to go to church to pray, I can pray at
home or anywhere." I like to ask, "Do you?...Do
you really give yourself a certain time out of the
day to pray, and if you do, how much time do you
give?"

We are morally responsible to take care of
our bodies and our souls and during this holy
time of Lent, we can get all the exercise we need
to be fit. There's physical activity in moving and

genuflecting at each Station of the Cross.

Walking is a great exercise going back and forth to daily Mass. Praying the rosary is a good way to gauge your power walk - it takes about fifteen minutes to pray one set of mysteries.

Regarding giving up various foods - remember, *diet is what we do for ourselves, fasting is what we do for God.* Please note, that any act of self-denial is good for the soul. It's healthy to say 'no' to ourselves with little things because it conditions us to say 'no' to the big things that can distance us from our God.

The third practice suggested by the Church for us to employ during Lent is alms sacrifice. Those little luxuries or delicacies we allow ourselves usually cost money, so perhaps while we are giving up those little things, we can use the money to give to better things. There are all kinds of charitable causes around us. Everywhere we look we will find a noble need for those dollars we spend on self-indulgence.

I must confess that I have already broken a couple of small resolutions I had for the new year, some of these habits are so much a part of me that I must constantly ask Our Lord for the grace to persevere. There's another prayer effort. Ask God to help you keep your resolutions. Then, don't give up, just give!

HOME
FOR THE HOLIDAYS

Everybody wants to be home for Christmas. It's a special time to spend with the special people in our lives and if we can't be home, we try to bring as much 'home' to where we are.

When I was in seminary in Rome, a small group of us always hung out together, an American, an Australian, and two Englishmen. Carl, the American, was very depressed because it was Thanksgiving Day and he was in Rome, in an English seminary and there was absolutely nothing happening, or even looking like a major holiday. He asked the rest of us to celebrate Thanksgiving with him and we said we were happy to do it, but we didn't know that we had to drive all over Rome looking for a restaurant that served up a Thanksgiving Day dinner. We couldn't find one. Finally, hungry and tired, we asked, "Carl, can't you just settle for CHICKEN...we're starved!" One look at his disappointed face and we knew the answer.

"I got an idea. Let's go to a butcher shop, and buy a turkey!" He said excitedly.

"Who's going to cook it?"... and more

103

importantly, "How long is it going to take?"

These were the questions he was hit with at the mere suggestion of buying a turkey. But he was relentless and talked us into going to the butcher's after he found a sympathetic cook at a restaurant we frequented.

We didn't sit down to Carl's Thanksgiving dinner until eleven o'clock that evening, but Carl had his turkey. In fact, that's all he had...just turkey. Somehow pasta as the side dish didn't meet the criteria for an authentic Thanksgiving meal.

Carl did the carving and the serving of the small turkey, but for someone who made such a big deal about "we have to eat turkey on Thanksgiving," he didn't look like he was enjoying himself. What was the problem? We couldn't figure this guy out.

While we were eating, he was mumbling about how right about now, back in Philadelphia, his family was probably sitting down to eat. They would have the table set with turkey, stuffing, yams, vegetables, cranberries, and the inevitable pumpkin pie. It would be a glorious meal, and afterwards, the men would go to the television and catch the football scores. The women would laugh and exchange stories while they cleaned up while the children would gather in one of the rooms and play some board game or cards.

Carl was getting more and more homesick, and although Thanksgiving didn't mean a thing to any of us since it is strictly an American custom, we found ourselves getting a little homesick too. It was the beginning of the holiday season and we were so very far from home. We began to appreciate Carl's need to connect somehow to his country and to his family traditions.

Holidays have a way of pulling us home, and making us feel like we want to go back to recapture the good feeling and happy family times we had together. It's sad, but true, that's how many Catholics think of Midnight Mass. They aren't there because they want to take part in the beautiful Christmas Liturgy and worship the Divine Babe, as much as they want to get back the feeling, the spirit of Christmas. Too often many arrive late for Midnight Mass and it doesn't take much discernment to know they already had too much Christmas 'spirits'!

Christmas traditions in England are quite different from here in the United States. In our home, FATHER CHRISTMAS, not Santa Claus leaves presents Christmas Eve and Midnight Mass was the focal point of the three-day celebration. It began with the whole family gathering together Christmas Eve and preparing for Mass. The children under eight had to stay home because Father Christmas would be coming soon. We put pillow cases at the end of our beds and hoped that Father Christmas would be generous...and he always was.

After we awoke on Christmas and found treasures, we went to Mass, then the whole day was one filled with celebration. There was always a huge meal followed by the ritual of the Plum Pudding. It began in the kitchen where brandy was poured over the moist cake and ignited. All the lights were turned out and Mum entered carrying the blue flamed pudding while we sang "Silent Night."

Christmas day was for celebrating Jesus' birthday. We didn't exchange our gifts until the day after Christmas, Boxing Day. In the states, it seems that once December 25 is over the celebration of Christmas ends, but at home it carries through to December 26th for that's when we give and receive presents from family and friends. In a way, I think it is better. Christmas is concentrating on Jesus' coming. The focus isn't on gifts, but rather, togetherness as we celebrate a member of our family's birthday, and important member, Jesus!

I still miss the Christmas celebrations from my childhood. You've heard the expression, "You can't go back." I think it's true. If I returned to England to try to recapture those memories, it would be depressing. Few of my family members are left and the rest are scattered all over and probably have created new family traditions. The parish Church, as I knew it growing up, no longer exists. Childhood friends have moved into different areas in England. Only one thing remains from the past, Midnight Mass.

We won't experience the Christmas Spirit until we commit ourselves to the Spirit of Christmas. It's more than fond memories, Christmas carols, parties and family gatherings. It's a preparation for Jesus' birth. Advent is the period the Church has set aside for preparation for the birth of Our Savior, a gestation period for us to appreciate God's tremendous gift to us, His Son,

Jesus. At Christmas, we will fully experience more joy singing "Oh come let us adore Him," if we really understand, "Oh come, Oh come, Emmanuel, and ransom captive Israel." Jesus came to set us free! Rejoice! Rejoice!

It's no secret that many Christians only attend Service or Mass at Christmas and Easter and as I said earlier, I think the gesture is more of an attempt to recapture memories and good feelings than an appreciation of the religious event and desire to give homage. People attend Church with the attitude; "I'm here Lord, aren't you glad? Now, make me feel good!" And you know what? He does.

Christmas Mass is the one event where we can return and find that things haven't changed so much after all. There may be a few liturgical prayers that have changed a bit, but it's still the same Scripture Readings, still the same Consecration, still the same Jesus coming to us in the Eucharist. Perhaps this is the only place where we can go home for the holidays and find what we're looking for...the Peace and Joy of Christmas.

OD'D ON O.J.

I guarantee that you cannot watch the television or listen to the radio for more than two hours and not be reminded of the horrific slaying of two people. Their deaths are a tragedy, but as bad, is the fact that these murders now take a back seat to the courtroom arena. The trying of this case has become a spectator sport - the prosecution vs. the defense. Each newscast gives you the score determined by which team scored the most points that day, and just in case you didn't figure it out for yourself, most stations have engaged a team of experts to advise you. Now it appears that everyone is centered on who is going to WIN, more than will justice prevail.

There is no escaping this legal circus. While standing in line at the grocery store, I guarantee there will be more than one tabloid displaying photos of the major players along with a sensational headline. Even at social get-togethers, you'll hear, "How do you think the trial is going?", or, "Do you think he did it?" Too, often, the answer is, "Yeah, but I think he'll get off."

It would be better to hear, "How very tragic that two people were brutally slain...we should pray for them and their families."

In the meantime, in a not very subliminal way, we are becoming desensitized to violence. The two slain people are not the only victims, so are we and so are the children.

The first time I was introduced to the Teenage Ninja Turtles, I had to ask, "Are they good or bad?" And when I first saw a Power Ranger, I had to ask it again. It was difficult because they all wore masks. Unfortunately, that is indicative of this whole phenomena; good and evil or not easily recognized. What confusion...especially to our young people.

While shopping one day with a friend who was picking up a birthday gift for his grandchild, I walked down one aisle in the toy department where these monster figures were displayed. They were frightening, grotesque figures that called something evil to mind. Kids are using these things for toys!

I did a little research in that store and discovered that there were more horrifying miniatures displayed than Disney characters. I saw several so called toys, that converted from cars to monsters. What for? This is what is being thrown at our young children. I find that pretty scary.

By the time they get to the teens, they graduate from toys to CDs. If you want a real scare, go to the music store and check out some of the CD covers and posters. They're bizarre! If you're brave enough, you might even want to listen to some of the music that has become so popular with our teens. Who puts the words to this (to use a broad term) "music"? In the old days, the use of this language was threatened with getting your mouth washed with soap. I would venture to say that many parents aren't aware of what the kids are listening to. The words are being obscured by the incessant beat and the end result is our kids are being saturated with violence and sexual promiscuity, and not always subliminally. They too, are being desensitized.

I remember way back when...if there was a murder in the city you talked about it for a week. Now, we listen to the evening news to hear about *how many* murders occurred the night before. What used to be abhorrent no longer shocks us. Frightening, isn't it?

Another thing I have observed, where have all the heroes gone? If the children consider the Teen-age Mutant Ninja Turtles and the Power Rangers their heroes, what's with the masks? It's obvious that evil is sometimes disguised as good, but why should we disguise good as evil? Is it because horror sells?

The next time you go to a video store, check out the number of horror films that line the shelves. There's a market for murder, terror and the occult. I find that fact *horrifying*.

So, what are we going to do about it? Parents, be vigilant about what movies your kids are watching and what kind of music they're listening to.   As adults, make choices. Give consideration to what brings out the best in you, whether it be television, programming, books, or conversation.

The greatest ammunition for the devil is apathy. Yes, I said, 'the devil.' By denying the existence of the devil in the world today, we are providing him with a fertile field to plant the seeds of evil that touch our daily lives. His influence is all around us.

The hype and merchandising of the OJ trial is just another example of the diabolical. Do you recall the first time you saw the bloody scene of the crime? Many of us gasped at the thought of two people savagely murdered at that bloody spot. Now, it has been flashed on the screen so often we rarely blink an eye, much less process the violence that happened there. The shock of the murders has been obscured by courtroom games and legal rhetoric, all volleying for our attention, and sometimes our dollars. You can dial a 900 number and ask questions about the defendant. You can purchase videos showing the crime scene, the sequence of events including the famous car chase, and parts of the trial itself. You can follow the courtroom proceedings everyday and be a part of a current poll that asks your opinion of the guilt or innocence of the defendant. You can even give your opinion about one of the prosecutor's current hairstyle. Or, you can 'judge' whether or not the judge is doing a good job, which attorney you favor, or, what the verdict will be. We have many choices.

We can also choose to pray. We can pray for the victims and their families. We can pray that justice will be served. We can pray for the Holy Spirit to grant His gift of discernment to the jurors. We can pray for some of that discernment for ourselves and our children. We can pray that we will not become desensitized to violence, and we can pray that we can recognize the diabolical. Evil wears many disguises!

To the reader...

This article was already printed before I learned of the movement to demonstrate against the Disney Corporation for producing a film that gave a very damaging image of the priesthood.

Please note that my reference to 'Disney characters' in this article was not an endorsement for some of what the corporation is producing now. Rather, it was used only to reference the beautiful fantasy world that has entertained and educated our children for years. I am sad that the corporation has chosen to violate the wholesome reputation Mr. Walt Disney had worked so hard to acquire for his company.

Fr. Ken

THE GRACE TO
KNOW YOUR GIFTS

Saint Paul compares the Church to a human body with many parts and he points out that all the parts are needed. " The eye cannot say to the hand, 'I do not need you'. Nor again the head to the feet, 'I do not need you." (1 Cor. 12: 21) Each one of us is important...each of us has a part to play.

My topic is grace. God supplies the necessary graces for the roles we are called upon to play in His Church. One may be a gifted song-writer, another a good listener, another may have the gift of knowledge or another, the power to preach. Still another may be a gifted administrator and so the list is endless. Even within a specific vocation such as priesthood, the gifts have corresponding graces and are varied.

I remember when I was just a newly ordained priest almost thirty years ago, I resided in a rectory with three other priests, one of whom didn't seem to have many obvious gifts. His Mass was very fast and not particularly inspirational, his confessional line was always very short, and his preaching seemed quite dull. He wasn't very popular with the parish team. I remember wondering why God even called him to priesthood. How very arrogant of me!

After I had been at this assignment for about six months, the priest in question went on vacation so the pastor asked me to fill in for him. "I'd be glad to, but what does he do?" I asked with a trace of sarcasm.

"He says Mass every morning, then visits the sick of the parish. He also goes to two hospitals and two nursing homes."

No big deal...or so I thought. I was about to discover to my horror what was NOT my gift. Visiting sick beds! Although God had given me the gift of the 'Blarney' and I was never at a loss for words when defending the Faith, I was completely speechless when I faced the patients who had tubes running in and out of them. What could I say to these suffering people?

I managed to stumble in and out of the first two visits then I looked down at the list to see how many were left, and my heart dropped. It would take me hours to go through all these sick people. God help me.

My plans were to get in and out as fast as I could and still fulfill the obligation. I would simply walk in, greet the person, introduce myself, give a blessing, and assure them of prayers. Then, I'd be out of there!

My plan was going pretty well until I came to this elderly lady, who was all propped up with pillows waiting for her visit. I went through my routine, smiled cordially and headed for the door when she stopped me. "Father, when will that nice priest be back?"

"Who?" I answered, not connecting a 'nice priest' to the one I was filling in for.

"The priest who usually comes here. He is so good, he always takes time to listen. When you get my age, Father, people assume you don't have much to say. It gets sort of lonely, but Father always makes me feel good. He always takes the time to listen...bless him!"

My mind was trying to process all that she said, I finally answered her question, "He will be back in about two weeks."

"Oh, thank God. I was so afraid that he may have been transferred." She continued, "You know, Father, he always seems so interested in all of us. And he takes the time to make us feel that he cares. I always pray for him. It must be difficult for him to always be looking after the sick and old people like myself." She smiled. "He has a gift!"

"Indeed he has." This time I answered with conviction and with a whole new appreciation of this priest. This dear old lady was right. Father did have a gift, one that I knew I didn't have. His ministry was filled with gifts. He brought the gift of consolation to all those to whom he ministered. Each day, he visited the sick bringing them the gift of Jesus in the Eucharist. He brought them the gift of Reconciliation and he brought them another precious gift, one that I had never appreciated before, the gift of just being there and listening.

The sick and old people he visited received many graces through this priest and he received many graces through his ministry. He was an example to me. He knew how to use his gifts to give and receive grace.

You too, are part of the Body of Christ. Which part are you? If you know this already, that is a grace and if you are ministering according to your gifts, you too are a bearer of graces.

If I can live without my legs, I would be handicapped....but I can live. Without eyes or hands, I don't want to and I would be handicapped...but I can still live. The Church can live without your gift, but she will be handicapped. She can exist without you, but she doesn't want to.

Use your gifts and be the bearer of graces.

CROSSROADS AND CROSSED WORDS

I feel like Mark Twain when he stated, "The report of my death was an exaggeration." Though I'm not aware of any stories going around that I am among the 'dearly departed,' some of the stories I have heard have been even more dramatic and much worse than death to me.

Permit me to explain. Recently, I have had to give more time to health problems which necessitated my canceling all my speaking engagements on the calendar, some of which had been booked for a couple of years. I can't tell you how reluctant I was to do this but my physician and spiritual director made it clear that there were no options if I was to have good health.

For over 15 years, I've been living out of a suitcase, sometimes traveling to three cities via the airlines, in a week's time. I was always packing, repacking, rushing to the airport, catching meals at sometimes, inappropriate times, and always putting routine medical check-ups on the bottom of my list of things to do. As a result, it caught up with me and I found myself experiencing aches and pains that I had never

117

had before. And I suppose, that along with my negligence of my health, I was negligent about respecting my years. This was brought home to me not so long ago when I was having dinner with a family who belonged to the parish where I was conducting a mission. While at the table, the topics of Social Security and Medicare benefits were being discussed due to the host's recent retirement. One of the guests turned to me and asked, "Are you eligible for Social Security yet, Father?"

For a second I was taken back. "Why, do I look that old?" I quipped, perhaps a bit defensively. Then it dawned on me. I WILL BE eligible in a very short time. I wondered how I came to be this old, this fast!

The conversation continued with all of us contributing how we were experiencing more physical limitations than we had in our younger days. Another guest remarked, "Father, I don't know how you do it. I could never keep your schedule... I just don't have the energy or the stamina anymore."

I answered, "Well, I don't really think about it."

"You're lucky, some of us have no choice," volunteered another guest. "But you really should get a good check-up...with the schedule you keep and all."

So, I decided to take their advice and made an appointment. While there, I learned I had dangerously high blood pressure. Something new, since it always had been low. Inevitably, I also discovered that I had dangerously high cholesterol, not surprising since I was one of those people, till then, that boasted about the fact that I had two eggs for breakfast almost every morning and got by with it. Not anymore.

I found I wasn't getting by with it after all. That "rosy" complexion which others had observed was probably just the result of the flush from the high blood pressure. That kink in my leg when I stood too long, or walked too much was in fact, a blocked artery. That little "touch of heartburn" was a hiatal hernia. And that newly acquired stiffness, occasionally accompanied by pain in my back and legs, was arthritis.

Certainly the mirror was not deceiving me when after each hair cut, the gray was becoming more and more visible, not to mention that the spots I observed on my hands were becoming larger in number and darker in color...and they weren't freckles!

The bottom line is simply I can't do what I used to do and maintain my health. This has been a hard pill to swallow...but I'm getting real good at swallowing pills. Never have I had so many of them! I had to accept the inevitable so I instructed my office to begin preparation for sending out letters canceling speaking engagements. Dictating the letters was a very difficult chore for me and hard for me to accept, but what has been happening since then is more difficult to accept.

It seems that somehow rumors have been erupting all around the country and coming back to my office. I don't understand how these stories get started but, thank God they aren't true.

The following are sample rumors:

Father Roberts has a terminal illness and he doesn't have long. Not true, thank God.

Father Roberts had a massive heart attack. Not true, but could happen if I don't change some habits.

Father Roberts had a stroke and he can't speak. Not true, still as 'preachy' as ever.

Father Roberts had quadruple bypass surgery. Not true, as long as I take care of myself.

Father Roberts is an alcoholic and he's been sent somewhere to dry out. Not true, drinking has never been a habit with me.

Father Roberts entered a strict Trappist monastery. Not true, but might be nice!

Father Roberts plans to go back to his native England. Not true, unless it's a vacation.

Father Roberts left the priesthood. Not true. I want to be buried in my priestly vestments when I die (which I don't predict will be in the near future from what they tell me.)

So, above is a sampling of what my office staff had to address in recent months. I can't help but wonder what else might be circulating out there that we can't correct.

This whole experience has made me aware of the virtue of prudence. When there is so much talk about 'stewardship', perhaps we should be more aware of being stewards of our speech. It's a fact that people often hear half of a story and embellish it. There have been actual tests to see how one sentence can be misheard, mistranslated or misunderstood when the line was whispered from one to another. At the end of the line, the statement is never the same when compared with the last person to the first person who started it. I'm certain it is even more so when it's a whole story.

There was some truth regarding my health problems, but not nearly as dramatic as the rumors have made them. It is true that I have been waging a battle with extremely high blood pressure for the past several months and it's true that I had angioplasty for a blocked vessel in my leg. And it is also true that I don't have the stamina to keep up the pace that had become my way of life for so many years. But I'm still a priest and I can still serve the Church through writing books, and making videos and tapes. The big difference in my ministry is that I will spend more time at my word processor and less time at airports. That's not all bad!

Fortunately I was able to correct some of the rumors that had been circulating. Yet, I couldn't help but get a new perspective on many people, especially my brother priests, who are not that fortunate. I remember just a few years ago, there was a rumor going around about a priest friend of mine (I'll not mention him by name for fear of perpetuating the rumor) who suffered greatly over a story about him being pulled in on a drunk driving charge. This never happened. It wasn't until months later, after the damage had been done, that it was discovered that someone by the same name had in fact, been guilty of this crime. The name was the same and somehow the story got around that it was my friend.

Another very fine, dedicated priest, became the victim of rumors started by a woman whom he counseled. He had refused to marry her and her fiance in the church because her first marriage was valid and had not been annulled. Her present fiance was a devout Catholic. When the couple broke up, the woman blamed the priest but I can only imagine it was more likely that the young man saw a different side of her when she displayed such resentment and anger. She wanted to destroy this priest...and almost succeeded.

Both incidents caused much suffering, but it would have never escalated to that point if people had not kept repeating what they had heard without any evidence that the stories were true.

I have a whole new appreciation of the story I'm about to tell you. I love it. I believe, and I hope I'm right because I've spent days trying to get someone to validate it, that it was St. Philip Neri who once said that if you stood in a field, ripped open a pillow and allowed the wind to scatter the feathers in all directions, it would be easier to retrieve every single feather than to trace and correct false gossip.

When you use that analogy, it most effectively demonstrates the far reaching consequences of idle gossip. And when that gossip is scandalous and damaging to another's reputation, it becomes sinful. We even have a commandment that addresses this issue, "Thou shall not bear false witness against thy neighbor." A reason to think twice before repeating a story that you don't know first hand to be true.

And even if you do know it to be true, is it worth harming another by repeating it in idle conversation? We can't judge what only God knows. Be patient. God isn't through with that person yet.

I must admit that I have been greatly moved by all the prayers that were offered in my behalf. And although my situation was not as serious as the rumors implied, the prayers must have been answered because my condition could very well have been more critical than it is.

I must take a line or two to thank the many people, some whom I knew and some whom I didn't, who called my office and wanted to know 'what was really going on.' It gave us the chance to set the story straight and it avoided one more story being repeated to someone else who repeated it to maybe two more, those two telling two more until one readily understands the pyramid scheme.

I have been a priest for almost thirty years as of this writing. It seems that these years since ordination have gone so quickly that I'm still amazed. If you want to really feel old, try being stopped by the father of a teenager who informs you that you conducted his EIGHTH GRADE RETREAT!

Suddenly retirement seemed very appropriate. I have suffered from the misguided notion that my stamina and energy, and even my physical fitness, would last forever. Not so.

But I am very much alive and active and spending hours and hours reading and writing. I feel just as committed and just as determined to serve the Church as I always have. I'm sharing this with you so that just in case, you are at your prayer group, or Ladies' Guild, or Men's Club and you hear some new 'information' about me and my ministry, you can be the one to give the 'real scoop,' which is: "Father Roberts is not dead yet, and from the looks of things he is going to be around for a long time. He is still very active in his ministry. Although he will be cutting back on public appearances, he will still be serving the Church through his writing."

When I look over my life since ordination, I feel so incredibly insignificant. So often throughout the years, I was foolish enough to think that I controlled my destiny, or to put it more accurately, I thought that I had a plan for my ministry and trusted God to help me see it through. But it hasn't been that way at all. God is the Planner, and sometimes without our even knowing it, He puts the people and the circumstances in our paths that often change our course. We will always know we're on the right road, when there is an inner peace.

It is with that inner peace that I am taking the turn that God's road signs are seeming to be leading me. Instead of racking up frequent flyer miles, it seems that I will be using up a lot of megabytes on my computer. And I have peace with that.

Thank you, God!

Part Two

Food for Thought...

by

Anna Marie Waters

IS ANYBODY HOME?

Have you noticed that people don't visit each other as much as they did years ago? I suppose television, busy schedules, two parents working, and climbing the social ladder, all have something to do with it. Still there was something folksy and comforting to know that we had a few people in our lives that we felt close enough to just drop in to say, "Hi," and exchange small talk. But it was more than small talk - it was saying we care and enjoy being with them. It wasn't unusual to hear a short knock at the door, hear the door open and a familiar voice say, "Is anybody home?" We don't seem to hear that much anymore, but you could easily ask that question when you enter some Catholic Churches that are unfamiliar to you.

There was a time when we walked into a Catholic Church we could recognize it immediately. We knew we would find a tabernacle, a sanctuary lamp, a crucifix, a few statues, a candle rack, and the stations of the cross lining the walls. Not true today.

There's been a big move to strip our churches of many of the things just noted, and I suppose some of these things are more comforting than essential. But that is not true of the tabernacle, the dwelling place for the Precious Host. The sanctuary lamp drew attention to the Blessed Sacrament reminding us of the Presence of our Lord and Savior. The crucifix was a visual reminder of the sacrifice He made for all of us.

Many of our Parish Churches have moved the Blessed Sacrament to an obscure place; they've removed the crucifix, often replacing it with some brass abstract sculpture that one would be hard pressed to identify. It seems to be more of a distraction than an inspiration. The change is explained by saying, "Christ has risen." We know that. But one can't fully appreciate the joy of the Resurrection until we understand the sacrifice at Calvary.

Something that we were all urged to do as long as I can remember, until recently, was the practice of making a visit to the Blessed Sacrament. Well, if you go into an unfamiliar Church, you may have to look around to find It and you may even be tempted to say, "Is anybody home?"

To "make a visit" was one of the things that made us Catholics feel so special - we had access. We could enter our Church and spend time with Jesus in the Blessed Sacrament. We could get away from our busy lives to be with Our Lord - and we were encouraged to do so. The practice, or non-practice, of making a visit was beautifully explained almost thirty years ago by Fr. Joseph Manton, CSSR in his book, *Straws From The Crib* published by Paulist Press.

"When Almighty God visited His subjects on this poor earth, He did much more than that. He actually became one of us: a human being - first in the cave of Bethlehem, a shivering Baby in a basket of straw; later on Calvary, that hill of blood and shadows, a gasping bleeding Man on a cross; and finally in the tomb, a gray, ashen corpse. You would think that this was enough, would you not? But not for Him! He loved us so much in order to remain among us, He even took the form of Bread - The Blessed Sacrament.

He showed His Love: do we show ours? They say the quietest and loneliest room in town is the morgue. I sometimes wonder if it is not a Church in the middle of the week. Rows upon rows perhaps of handsomely carved pews: stained glass windows blazing with fiery beauty; maybe the shafts of sunset laying rainbows upon the marble floor - and a congregation of statues, of Stations, of pictures! Outside, so many cars go whizzing by, so seldom one draws up. Outside, so many footsteps go hurrying past, so seldom any turn in.

> *So few there come to visit Him*
> *The long and lonely day,*
> *You'd think the flame-red altar light*
> *meant DANGER! KEEP AWAY!"*

128

PROMISES, PROMISES

There's something very sacred about a promise. It's a vow. And promises are to be taken seriously, especially when children are concerned. When my children were small and I told them that we were going to do something that they really looked forward to, they would often challenge me with, "Do ya promise?" Believe me, I had better make certain I would carry out my intentions or they called me to accountability. If something important happened that kept me from fulfilling my intentions, there was no way of explaining priorities because children aren't wise enough to determine what is or is not important. All they would answer in disappointment, was, "...BUT YOU PROMISED!" I learned quickly in the parenting game never to make a promise I wasn't certain that I could keep. It represented more than a disappointment, it was a breech of trust.

Another thing about promises, we use them as bargaining tools, "If you do this for me, I promise I'll do that for you." We even do it in our prayer life. "Lord, if you will grant me this favor, I promise I will go to Mass more often."

Or maybe we bargain with Our Blessed Mother, "If you will obtain this favor for me, Mary, I promise to say a rosary each day."

Children don't have a monopoly on expecting promises to be fulfilled. All of us are hurt when we feel a promise has been broken and our trust has been betrayed. It's pretty much the same feeling we get when we keep begging God for something and when it doesn't happen, we feel our prayers are unanswered. As we have all heard many times...*God always answers our prayers, but sometimes He says,* "No!" He can determine best our need, not what we *think* we need, and as time passes, we discover that God's plan was better than ours.

Children have the right to expect their parents to fulfill their promises and we have a right to expect God to fulfill His. When we doubt that for a moment, our faith is tested. A great illustration of this is in a story a friend shared with me several years ago. She was talking about her father's sudden death when she was only twenty-two years old.

Her dad was from Ireland and the Catholic Faith was as much a part of him as his arms and legs. He practiced and believed with everything in him the devotion to the Sacred Heart of Jesus and the twelve promises made to St. Margaret Mary. He never, never missed a 'first Friday.' (Is this a blast from the past, or what?) No matter what the weather, or circumstances, he was there for Mass every first Friday of the month. If the family was on vacation, or no matter how inconvenient driving miles out of the way to find a Catholic

Church and Mass on that day, John Carrol was there. When questioned about his determination, and sometimes, borderline stubbornness about this, he answered, "Our Lord promised a priest will be there at the hour of our death!" He was fixed.

But John Carroll's death did not come in the warmth of a bed with his family around him, rather, while he was making a delivery in his truck, he suffered a fatal heart attack and was pronounced dead when the ambulance arrived to take him away. This news was devastating to his family. His wife and his only child felt John had been betrayed and left to die alone in the cold streets of an apathetic city.

When the family received the news, his wife immediately asked if a priest tended to her husband. It was the City Hospital and as she feared, no priest was present because he was, as they put it, *dead on arrival*. John's wife and daughter grieved not only for the loss of their husband and father, but also for the promise that he believed throughout his whole life...that a priest would be with him at the hour of his death. Still, no consolation came. "Sorry, Mam, I didn't see any priest...we just picked him up and took him to City Hospital."

The feelings of grief were being invaded by thoughts of resentment, and certainly doubts about faith in a God Who was supposed to keep His promise. Throughout the two-day ordeal of a wake and subsequent funeral, the family went through all of the motions still haunted by John's misplaced confidence that God would give him the grace of the Sacrament of the Last Rites at his hour of death. It was a hard pill to swallow.

After the funeral, the typical Irish gathering following the burial, my friend and her mother were alone in their home. The feeling of loss and doubt swelled when the rest of the family and friends left them. They felt abandoned by John Carroll, abandoned by family and friends...and because of the circumstances surrounding John's death, abandoned by God. Their grief was broken by the sound of a telephone ring. When John's daughter, Mary, answered, she heard, "Is this the family of the John Carrol who is recently deceased?"

Mary answered affirmatively then the caller identified himself as a Catholic priest. He explained that it had taken a while for him to track down what happened a couple of days ago, but he wanted them to know that he was driving down the street when he saw a man get out of his truck and fall. He stopped his car and directed a bystander to call an ambulance. He asked the man if he was a Catholic and went immediately to his car to get his stole and holy oils. John Carroll had made his confession, received the anointing and was very much at peace...even joy, before the ambulance took him away.

The ambulance driver never had a clue that the young man who was holding the hand of his passenger when they took him away, was a priest. It was the young priest's day off and he was dressed to attend a parish picnic.

There are two lessons in this story: let's talk more about devotion to the Sacred Heart of Jesus and resurrect the devotion of the First Fridays; and the other lesson...GOD ALWAYS KEEPS HIS PROMISES!

THE TWELVE PROMISES OF OUR LORD TO ST. MARGARET FOR THOSE DEVOTED TO HIS SACRED HEART

I will give them the graces necessary in their state of life.

I will establish peace in their homes.

I will comfort them in all their afflictions.

I will be their secure refuge during life, and above all in death.

I will bestow a large blessing upon all their undertakings.

Sinners shall find in My Heart the source and the infinite ocean of mercy.

Tepid souls shall grow fervent.

Fervent souls shall quickly mount to high perfection.

I will bless every place where a picture of My Heart shall be set up and honored.

I will give to the priests the gift of touching the most hardened hearts.

Those who shall promote this devotion shall have their names written in My Heart, never to be blotted out.

I promise thee in the excessive mercy of My Heart that My all-powerful love will grant to all those who communicate on the First Friday in nine consecutive months the grace of final penitence; they shall not die in my disgrace nor without receiving the sacraments; My Divine Heart shall be their safe refuge in this last moment.

GENERATION GAP...
OR CRUNCH?

I have survived the generation gap, that period when I couldn't relate to my parents, then later when my children couldn't relate to me! My children have become young adults and thankfully, we are able to communicate better. We have graduated in age and hopefully, some wisdom, whereby now we have a mutual respect for each other. Thank you, God.

Although I no longer experience the confusion of the generation gap, I have reached the age of what I call the "generation crunch," that space in our lives when our parents need more of our time, more of our understanding, and very often, more of our patience. All my life, I have gone to them for advice, affirmation, support and comfort, and now they are seeking these same commodities from me.

God has blessed me by allowing me to have my parents so long, and may I add, to really *enjoy* my parents so long. It has only been lately that I have seen the predictable signs of aging with my folks. I'm not talking about gray hair and wrinkles, I'm referring to a slower step; once in a while a little confusion; often a great deal of fatigue, and gradually I have watched their health decline. We seem to be spending more money on medicine than entertainment. And a great deal of our conversations are about health matters. I also find myself repeating directions or a story because they didn't hear all of it, or maybe didn't grasp it as quickly as they once did. Being the great parents they have always been, they keep affirming me by letting me know how much they appreciate whatever I do..and they hasten to add, "We hate to take up so much of your time." It's ironic since *time* was the precious commodity they have always given to me.

They were never too busy to listen to what I had to say, whether it was a story I brought home from school, later from my job, and finally, about my own children. Incidentally, they could never hear enough about my kids since I'm *the only child*, my children were their only grandchildren. They made me feel that whatever I had to say was important. Now I find myself wanting to make them feel the same way. I have reached the age, like many others, where we find ourselves 'parenting' our parents.

Recently, my parents, two aunts, and I had to make a major decision about a nursing home for another of my mother's sisters. It was very traumatic. My ailing aunt had no children and had been widowed for many years. Her health was failing rapidly and she could no longer live independently so the doctor advised us that it was time for a skilled nursing facility. We accepted the inevitable and set out to find the best nursing home as close to all of us as possible so visiting would be more accessible. The quest for a "nice" nursing home is probably one of the most heart-wrenching experiences that many of us will have to experience. No matter how expert the care and clean the facility, there still prevails that quiet sadness and the awesome reality of aging.

There's food for a thousand hours of meditation inside each nursing home. One can't help but come face to face with his or her own mortality. If we are fortunate, perhaps sometimes, unfortunate, to live that long, we will have to depend on others for our basic needs. Priorities shift. Things that once were important to us no longer exist.

It never ceases to amaze me how Our Lord knows our needs...I'm certain He knows mine. I have always dreaded the thought of losing my parents, and as I watch them age, I want to grasp time and make it stand still because the inevitable is closing in on me. Still, I feel Our Lord is preparing me to let go. My mother often talks about her death and tells me her only prayer is that she will never be a burden to anyone, that God will bring her home before her care would interfer with my life. What a mom!

My dad says he hopes to meet his Maker while watching a baseball game or opening a six-pack! (Dad's way of saying that he too, doesn't want to be a burden. He's saying the same thing, but more colorfully, I might add.)

I'm certain that many of you readers are sharing this generation crunch, and maybe at times you feel your're being pulled apart by not only the needs of husbands or wives, your children or grandchildren, but the more immediate needs of parents. Perhaps you can look upon this time as a preparation for your own aging process and gather the grace that comes with these special times. It's an exercise in patience, understanding, and most of all, love, the very commodities our parents have so generously given to us!

CAN WE TALK?

Recently I wrote an article addressing a very sensitive subject, the care of aging parents. It must have struck a nerve because there was a lot of reaction. My friend, Mary, also an only child, cares for her mother and a maiden aunt, both well into their eighties, who live with her. Mary said she really related to the piece I wrote because she certainly feels the *generation crunch*. But she went on to suggest that one of the best ways to deal with this situation, "You gotta keep a sense of humor."

I responded with, "But Mary, it's pretty difficult to find something to laugh about when you watch people you love decline physically and intellectually."

Her answer triggered a conversation that found me drying my eyes, not crying tears, but laughing tears. It began with, "Listen Annie, there's sadness all over the place, injustices, violence, catastrophes. Some people go to their rooms and fret, but that doesn't change it. I think that's why God gave us a sense of humor."

She added, "It's like when I die, I'm going to ask God, 'Can we talk?' because I got a whole lot of questions to ask God, and the first one is going to be, 'What were you thinking about when you created calories? I mean...do we really need them, Lord? And what about liver spots...now, was that really necessary?...Not to mention arthritis, diets, hairy legs, split ends and cellulite!'"

Before we knew it, we were laughing and what began as a somewhat somber conversation, became a simulated comedy routine. Maybe that is the key to coping. Release that stress pressure valve with a good laugh. I'm certain that's why God gave us a sense of humor.

Not all of us can be witty, but all of us can learn to laugh, especially at ourselves. Laughter is downright therapeutic. It's really ironic when you think about it. Some of the occasions I have laughed the hardest were times when the situations were really quite sad.

For instance, years ago, my cousin Kathleen and I met to go to a wake. We were around nineteen years old, still young enough and blessed enough that we had little experience about visiting a funeral home. Our parents, in their wisdom and compassion, said it wasn't necessary for us to spend a great deal of time there, as was their intention, however, our brief appearance was appropriate and expected. The deceased was a very close friend of our family and his daughter who was our age was a girlfriend of ours.

I picked up Kathleen and the mood was sad, both of us feeling sorry for our friend's loss. As we approached the funeral home, Kathleen was becoming more anxious.

"What are we going to say?...I don't know what to say."

"We just say we're sorry, I guess," I answered.

"What's that word everybody uses...you know the one that begins with a 'C'?"

"I don't know, all I can think of is 'sorry', or 'sympathy'," I replied.

Kathleen insisted, "No. No. There's a special word that everybody uses when they go to a funeral home...what is it?"

"Condolences!" Suddenly, it dawned on me.

"That's it...Condolences!"

So, she began to rehearse, "You have my *condolences...condolences....*"

Finally we arrived at the funeral home, Kathleen was still rehearsing, "Condolences, Condolences." We entered the room where the casket was displayed; the widow stood by it sadly gazing down. Suddenly Kathleen bolted ahead of me, took her hand, and in a more than audible voice bellowed, "Congratulations!"

I was horrified and wanted to run from the room, instead I just stood there dumbfounded. Poor Kathleen was mortified and about to break out in tears due to embarrassment more than grief. Suddenly, the widow began laughing, but seeing how devastated Kathleen was she tried to console her. "It's okay dear, for the last two days I didn't think I would ever laugh again. Mr. Welby would have loved it. Thank you."

Kathleen's faux pas broke the tension. The gift of a sense of humor coupled with a lot of faith is what gets us through our trials. Nobody escapes life without some grief. Suffering is a part of living...which brings us to another speculation. If Eve had not given into the temptation in the garden of Eden, would we have really been spared all this?

According to my friend, Mary, she intends to investigate. "After I ask God all those questions I have pondered all my life, I'm going to search around heaven, assuming that Eve made a good act of contrition. I'm going to look for a woman without a navel and when I find her, I've got a few questions for her too. 'How could you? If it had been a pizza, or a cheesecake, maybe a hot fudge sundae...but an *apple!*'"

God uses all things.

HAPPY BIRTHDAY, LITTLE JESUS

I love Christmas! In my home, if something doesn't move, I decorate it.

When my children were still in grade school, even in high school, I woke them up every morning by playing Johnny Mathis' Christmas album. This ritual began the Monday after Thanksgiving; from then on, every morning, they woke up to, "Sleigh bells ring, are you listening?" It was a lively tune that I always hoped would get a lively response. As soon as they were on their feet and motivating, I turned the album to the other side and played Christmas carols. That's how they began their days during Advent - it got them going. We ended the day by lighting the Advent wreath...there was no way I wanted them to forget what all this preparation and celebration, was about.

When they were small (and they were all small at the same time because all five were born in six years) I read them the Gospel of Matthew from the Children's Bible. It was in their language and they loved the story, so did I because I knew that each time they saw a Nativity scene

142

during the holidays, they knew what it meant.

Children are great little people. They're never bored with something they enjoy. Just ask any parents who have the *Beauty and the Beast* video; kids want to watch it over and over again. So it was with my little ones. After the dinner clean-up, they were always ready to hear all about Jesus' birthday. They knew the story so well; I could stop in the middle of a sentence and they would finish it. When Mary and Joseph found the stable and Jesus was born in the manger, they would clap their hands and say, "Yea!" as if they were hearing it for the first time. They were never tired of hearing about Jesus' birth and they were always coming up with new ideas about what to give Him for His birthday. I told them that what Jesus wanted most was for them to be kind to each other, not to fight, to share their toys, to mind their mom and dad, to say their prayers, to be good at Mass and so on. These were the things that I suggested but their ideas were far more creative.

One said he wasn't going to stick out his tongue at the little girl next door; another said he was going to throw his dirty clothes in the clothes hamper because that was being *nice* and he would eat all his supper so "nobody would get mad at him." My oldest daughter said she would share her bows with her sister and not make her cry anymore. We all agreed that these were very kind things to do that would make Jesus happy on His birthday. Just as the kids were predicting the words of the story, so I could predict their responses about what they were going to do for

Baby Jesus. I always finished our little sessions by reminding them how much Jesus cared about them, that He would always be there to help them because He loves them *so very, very much.* We lit our Advent wreath then off they would go to play just a little longer until it was time for bed. I'll admit that often watching them scamper away I would mentally pat myself on the back like "Little Jack Horner." *See what a good Mom am I!*

Children have a tremendous talent for bringing you back to reality without even knowing it; they can get to the heart of the matter and they become the teacher. The incident I'm about to share with you has become indelible in my mind, one of those parenting experiences that I will always cherish.

It happened during one of the our Advent evenings. The kids had once again applauded Jesus' birth and predictably we went through the litany of nice things to do for Jesus for His birthday. Four of the children responded until it was Johnny, my five year-old's turn, but he said nothing.

"Johnny, what are you going to do for Jesus?," I asked patiently (almost sweetly.)

"This is stupid...I don't want to talk about it!"

With that sharp answer, he arrogantly walked away and headed down the hall toward his room. I wanted to call after him, no, *yell* after him, "Get back here, young man!" but I didn't want to spoil this warm fussy time for the rest of the kids, so I ignored him and continued to talk to the others for a few more minutes. We sang a Christmas carol, hugged and off they went. I headed straight for John!

Give me patience, Lord. I know I get through to the other kids, but why is Johnny so difficult? I started toward the boys' room, but I never made it that far. Johnny was in the hall, sitting with his legs crossed, Indian fashion and huddled forward. He had the crucifix that hung in his room in his lap. I was confused and more than surprised because the cross had been placed so high on the wall that I knew he had to negotiate climbing on top of his chest of drawers to get it. I didn't know what to reprimand him for first; his behavior during our Christmas story time, or climbing to get the crucifix down. In a loud, scolding tone, I asked, "Johnny, what do you think you're doing?"

He look up at me sadly, "I just wish I could do something to make His hands and feet feel better!"

Wow, what do I say now, Lord?

I learned a lot that evening; never to underestimate children and to always remember how impressionable kids are. That's why it's so very important to monitor what we say in their presence. We never know what their reaction will be and they don't always tell us. As for underestimating...I thought Johnny was not interested and belligerent, when really, he was processing his own thoughts and feelings. Johnny was not only aware of Jesus' love for him, he *felt* close enough to want to make his friend "feel better." Johnny looked past the manger, to the cross.

There is no better time of the year to introduce children to Jesus and how much He loves them. Perhaps, that's true for us grown-ups, too. During mental prayer, as we answer the call to "Come let us adore Him," meditate on this tremendous gift: "God so loved the world that He sent His only Begotten Son."

ANGLES ON ANGELS

Once in a while, something so spectacular happens in our lives and try as we may, we just can't explain it. Until I had the personal experience I'm about to share with you, I became a little agitated by people who would say things such as "I'm asking *my angel* to help me." Or perhaps, it would be something like, "YOU SHOULD ask your guardian angel...."

I've always had this urge to say, "Grow up!" I hadn't said that *guardian angel prayer* since I was a kid. It was cute and appropriate then but I wanted to think that I graduated in my spirituality since grade school. I was very contented to let the little angels take care of the little kids. I was more into *fiat*, "thy will be done!" Now, that's not all bad but once in a while the child in us cries out in desperation. Such was this incident...

It happened almost twelve years ago and it involved my maiden aunt, Aunt Jen. She was one of those dear souls who always put her needs last. Her very life was a study of unselfishness. She chose to remain single and care for her parents until they died, but her caring far exceeded them, she cared for and about everybody, especially her family. Being the first niece, I admit I was spoiled by her lavish gifts. It was her practice to always provide me with a stylish Easter outfit. It was a ritual I always looked forward to. We got on the big bus that went all the way downtown, then we went to the finest shops, no department stores for us! It was she who gave me my first watch, a wonderful Mickey Mouse watch that I treasured for years until she felt that I had graduated into something more sophisticated, a silver Bulova with dainty numbers and a beautiful raised crystal. I brandished this timepiece with the fervor of a prospective bride with a new engagement ring. It was my thirteenth birthday gift and I loved it. Like the Mickey Mouse watch, I treasured it for many years.

Aunt Jen worked at the same factory job from the time she was twelve until she retired at sixty-five. She was a diligent worker who took pride in everything she did. The activity she enjoyed most was singing in the church choir, and she was good at it. After my grandmother died, she lived alone for the next thirty years until her death at the age of seventy eight. She was beautiful even in her old age, on the outside as well as the inside.

She had been diagnosed with a terminal illness. The malignancy had metastasized into her bones and moving her was painful. The doctor advised a nursing home for her remaining days; I chose one just a couple of blocks from my home so I could be close to her. I was working at

a job also not far from my home so it was easier
to see her often.   I looked in on her after seven
o'clock Mass before I went to work.   I often
stopped in on my lunch hour and always after
work each day. She was only there nine weeks
before she died, but because I spent so much time
at the home, I became friendly with the nursing
staff.

Many hours were spent in silence because
the pain medication allowed her to sleep, but
when she was awake we talked about the weather,
the old days, our family, my children and her
friends from church.   She never, never
complained about her condition and her rosary
was always in her hand. She seemed to get
strength from her beads. God knows, I did.

Toward the last, I became more aware of
how important it was to her to have someone
close by. I thought that was interesting since she
had lived alone so much of her life, yet she never
complained about being lonely. The awareness of
her days being numbered stirred up a lot of guilt
in me. Why hadn't I spent more time with her
during my adult years? Sure, I called her
routinely and visited at least once a month and
for all the major get-togethers and holidays she
was included, but now I wanted to roll back the
years and be there with her more. She always
understood that raising five kids took a lot of
time...but could I have done more? Could I have
just set aside more time for Aunt Jen? Whatever
the answer, I vowed I would be present to her
now...I would be there every moment I could.

It became more and more obvious that the

end was near so I asked the nurses to keep my work number and home number at the desk and to call me at any time, day or night, if her condition began to decline. They kept their promise.

It was around noon on a Monday when I received the call at work, "Your aunt has declined considerably in the past few hours and her breathing has become very labored. We thought you should know."

I had seen her before I went to work and I was afraid she may be slipping into a coma because she didn't respond when I spoke to her, but the nurse explained the medication may be responsible for that. Now, it seemed my fears were justified, so I asked my supervisor if I could take one of my week's vacation. My aunt needed me to be there... or maybe, I needed to be there more.

It was not pleasant. Very little of the time when her eyes were open was she able to communicate. Sometimes she would give a gesture or a smile. It almost seemed as if she were comforting me. They told me she could go at any time. She had already developed that sound that resembled crinkly cellophane from her throat. I begged God to be gentle and bring her home, but the hours dragged into days. I kept a vigil by her bed leaving her only to go to Mass or to run home to shower and change.

On Thursday afternoon that week, I felt emotionally drained and I was filled with a thousand questions. She seemed to be resting a bit so I went to my parish church. My mood was not prayerful, rather I was angry. "Why God? Why do you allow her to suffer like this? Why? Why? Why?" I became frantic. "God, You're not listening! Mother Mary, aren't you interceding? Where is everybody?"

I slumped in the pew and began to cry. I couldn't come up with any answers and I even began to doubt all that I was taught, and believed, about a loving God. In desperation, I cried out, "She's been alone so much of her life, don't let her die alone." I implored all of heaven to intercede for me. And something that I hadn't done since I was a child, I prayed to my guardian angel, and her guardian angel. Finally, I left the church and returned to Aunt Jen's bedside feeling that maybe my trip to church had been in vain. My faith was shaken. I was confused...and I was filled with doubt.

I stayed at the hospital until about nine that evening. I wanted to shower and get ready for another long night. When I returned home, Fr. Ken was visiting with my husband. I explained that I couldn't stay, that I had to get back to my aunt. My husband tried to persuade me to take a night off and stay at home to get some interrupted sleep. I wouldn't hear of it.

Fr. Ken offered to go with me and spend the night in prayer. *A lot of good that's going to do,* I thought. But I welcomed the company so I accepted the offer. On the way to the hospital, Father told me of my husband's concern about my obsession with this whole situation. He was afraid it was getting to me. He advised me to consider my own health and the worries of my family. Predictably, he offered, "Trust God." Yeah, right!

We began our vigil. Aunt Jen had already received the Sacrament of the Sick so Father started the rosary. Hours later, Aunt Jen was still the same. Finally, at 4:40 a.m., Father said he would have to be going since he had the six o'clock Mass and he wanted to freshen up. I felt guilty keeping him up all night so I offered to get him some coffee and a quick breakfast before he returned to the rectory. I told the nurse I was leaving, but I would be back in a few hours. "Go home and sleep...your aunt's condition hasn't changed and this could go on for a couple of days. I promise to call you if anything changes."

Tension gave way to exhaustion. We went into the living room. Father sat in the recliner claiming to "rest his eyes" for a few minutes before he had to leave to say Mass. I spread out on the couch. It was 5:05 a.m. Instantly I was asleep until I felt a gentle push on my shoulder.

"What?" I bolted up. "What is it, Father?"

"I didn't say anything, Ann." He looked bewildered.

"But you pushed my shoulder."

"No, Ann. You must have been dreaming. Go back to sleep."

I realized there was no way he could have been near enough to touch my shoulder then return to the recliner across the room. "I can't sleep...I've got to go." I was on my feet, grabbed my purse and out the door. As I got in my car, Father was calling out to me, "Ann, this is crazy, you must sleep!"

I had to go to the rear entrance of the nursing home where the deliveries are made since the front doors were closed during the night. When I rang the bell, Betty, the night nurse, opened the door for me. "Honey, you should stay home and get some rest. I just looked in on your aunt and she's fine. She's just the same."

I walked past her into Aunt Jen's room. Her eyes were fixed, but she seemed to be resting better. Even her breathing was not as labored. "I'm back, Aunt Jen." I began the rosary again because I knew if she could hear, it would comfort her. Besides, it would give me something to do.

I began the first Sorrowful Mystery, the Agony in the Garden, I heard a gentle sigh from my aunt. Her breathing stopped. It was over. She died...but not alone. I was there.

That gentle touch on my shoulder brought me out of a sleep and to her bedside. I can't begin to tell you the peace that came over me at that moment and I knew like never before, the presence of the angels. I don't know if it was my guardian angel, or Aunt Jen's guardian angel that got me to her at the time of her death, but I do know God heard my prayer and answered it in a special way. Perhaps I needed that much drama to rekindle devotion to my guardian angel.

Since that time I have become more aware that often things we cannot explain is indeed very explainable. I have heard many stories that seemed to credit divine intervention for allowing someone to escape something that could have been very harmful and very often these stories have come from individuals who ask protection

and guidance routinely from his or her guardian
angel. We should never outgrow the prayer we
learned as children...

> *Angel of God, my guardian dear,*
> *To whom God's love commits me here.*
> *Ever this day be at my side,*
> *To light, to guard, to rule and guide.*

I know someone *guided* me.

THE *EYES* HAVE IT!

I was privileged to make a retreat at a monastery. It was so beautiful; the grounds, the chapel, the music, the retreat talks, the liturgies, and the magnificent singing. If you closed your eyes you felt as if the heavens opened and all you could hear was a choir of angels. Well, actually it was a choir of angels, figuratively speaking...it was the nuns from Our Lady of the Angels Monastery in Birmingham, Alabama. This is the home of the Eternal Word Television Network, the one and only Catholic Cable Station.

If I were asked to describe what impressed me most about this place, I could sum it up in one word. JOY! It surrounds you. Everybody down there, the priests, the brothers, the nuns, the extern sisters, the camera crew, the people who open the mail, the office staff, just everybody...their witness is joy. It shows in their eyes.

I tried to explain this to my family and a few of my friends when I returned from my retreat, but I'm afraid I just couldn't do it justice. It's like when someone gets some wonderful news that they've been waiting for, or how a bride looks on her wedding day, or a new mom and dad when they see their new baby for the first time. There's a happiness that shows on their faces.

If you have ever watched the faces on the nuns at the televised Masses on EWTN when the camera pans them and occasionally closes in on a single face, you know what I mean. There's a peace and reverence that is hard to explain...but it's in the eyes.

This look doesn't just belong to the nuns, you can see it on the priests and brothers. I met one young man, an aspirant, who had the most contagious smile I have ever experienced. I told him he should be on a vocation poster. His obvious happiness at the prospect of giving his life to God would spark the curiosity of many young people. This young man's eyes danced with the excitement of serving the Lord. And to all of us who have realized our vocation, married, single, priesthood, or religious, his smile is a reminder of the peace and joy that comes with seeking God's will.

I don't know who once said, "The eyes are the windows of the soul," but the quotation became more meaningful after my visit to the Monastery. The serenity in the eyes of the people there is a result of staying focused...and the whole focus of this monastery is Jesus in the Blessed Sacrament.

The fact that Mother Angelica has successfully accomplished the almost impossible feat of having a Catholic Cable Network is not an accident. It's the power that comes with perpetual adoration.

It pains me to hear her criticized by so many who say she's old-fashioned or out of step with the needs of the Church today. I don't understand that. What does she and her sisters promote? What is so subversive about traditional habits? What is so threatening about staying loyal to Church Doctrine? Is she to be chastised for supporting the Holy Father? And when she constantly emphasizes devotion to Our Lord in the Blessed Sacrament...who can find fault with that? She and her sisters are dedicated to Perpetual Adoration, the teachings of the Church, devotion to the Mother of God, prayer, the sacraments, loyalty to the Holy Father and inspirational Catholic programming. So, what is the focus of those who oppose her?

I don't even want to speculate about that. No, rather, I want to hold on to the peace and joy I experienced at Our Lady of the Angels Monastery. It was "the pause that refreshes," and the best part is, all of us can get a taste of it each time we spend time before the Blessed Sacrament. Mother Angelica and the nuns are not keeping their formula for beautiful eyes a secret!

"BUT IT WAS <u>MARY</u>... LONG BEFORE THE FASHION CAME"

When asked to write something about the Blessed Mother, I found myself at a loss for words. It's certainly not because I have no devotion to her. On the contrary, her intercession has brought me through every crisis in my life, and since I was old enough to learn the HAIL MARY, I have felt a need to go to her for prayer...just as I have always done with my own mother. There's a reason for that - like my own mother, I know she will always listen.

There was a time after the Second Vatican Council, because of misinformation or the lack of education, many parishes played down Marian devotion...some eliminated it all together (and some, sadly, have not picked it up again). It seemed to be the fashion to no longer include Mary. We all became very intellectual and began to read more about our faith. We depended more on our heads and less on our hearts.

We mothers were not about to give up our patron. I remember in the late sixties, clutching my rosary while I was awaiting the birth of my fifth child to make her grand entrance (or should I say, *exit?*) when my OB walked in the labor room and teasingly said, "Haven't you heard? The rosary is out...liturgy's in!" I answered that I was hardly in a position to have liturgy, but God knew how much I needed my mother at that moment.

But I'm not alone. A dear friend of mine who always classified herself as a 'progressive' Catholic, admitted that any time she was faced with an urgent matter, it was almost like a reflex that she began to pray the HAIL MARY. She was certain it was because of her parochial educational background, but I'm not so sure. I think it was the Holy Spirit reminding her that she had a prayer partner who was always there for her.

I'm not equipped to dazzle you with all the theological reasons or quote all the Scripture passages that validate Mary's role in the Church, but I would like to tell you about Our Lady's intercession in my growing-up years.

I'm really dating myself by sharing with you my memories of grade school when we had the annual May Procession. All of us girls couldn't wait to get to the eighth grade so our names could be put in the box to be drawn to see who would be the one to crown the Blessed Mother. I must admit, the fact that we were allowed to wear a long formal dress (usually the same one we had for grammar school graduation) was also a great incentive. After all, we were thirteen!

Well, my name wasn't drawn and I was crushed. I was so certain that Our Lady would see to it because she knew how much I wanted it. Not only did I not get picked to be the queen, I didn't even get picked to be one of the maids (who also wore long formals). It wasn't fair. Joann (the one who was picked) never made as many visits as I did. And Catherine, Minette, Janice and Betty, the maids, never stayed after school as I did to help Sister Mary Sabina organize the Living Rosary. I felt like any child who wants something so badly, but Mother says, "No." All the dreams I had to be the one who would crown our Lady were shattered and I really fought back the tears. I was so certain I would be the one. Blessed Mother never failed me before...

As we were about to close the planning meeting, Sister closed her notebook and said, "Anna Marie, you can carry the banner." And that was that. Well, at least it was something, and although my enthusiasm was gone, I knew that qualified me to wear a formal.

Finally, came the day of the procession. We took our places and I was the one who would lead the procession from the school into the Church. Sister handed me this long wooden pole that supported the baby blue satin banner on which was painted a picture of Jesus. It was so beautiful. It was a gentle picture of Jesus with His arms outstretched as if to draw me closer to Him. I was blessed. Never before had I felt so close to Our Lord and Our Mother. At thirteen, I learned in an indelible way what Mary's role is. She always brings us to her Son!

I still get choked up when I hear, ON THIS DAY, OH BEAUTIFUL MOTHER, and MOTHER DEAREST, MOTHER FAIREST, and I wish we could sing them more often. It's good that there is a rebirth of Marian devotion because as Catholics, we must never apologize for our devotion to the Mother of God.

You know...whenever someone gives us a gift, it is not his or her intention that we should cast it aside. On the contrary, a gift should be cherished.

And Our Dear Lord gave us His Mother.

BIG JOHN

His name was John W. Ruskin. Ruskin wasn't his real last name. Way back when he was a very young man, it became his nickname. It seems there was this horse named Ruskin; John liked the name and he liked the horse. The fact that John smoked cigars and there was a brand of cigars called, JOHN RUSKIN CIGARS, the name sort of attached itself to him. People began to refer to him as John Ruskin and it stuck so much so, that finally, later in life he made it legal since more people identified him with that name.

John was born John Walter Ruszkowski; Ruskin was less complicated, easier to pronounce and certainly easier to spell. But John never felt that he was denying his Polish nationality...NEVER! He was proud to be Polish and in his home that was the language that was spoken. Both his parents were immigrants from Poland and like many other Poles, they were very loyal to their homeland as well as their faith. John boasted about how faithful Polish people have always been to their Church, and he often joked, "The reason Poland never won a war is because they had too many priests and not enough

162

soldiers!"

John was a man of simple tastes. He was not an adventurer. In fact, he never traveled out of the state of Missouri or Illinois. He had never even been as far as Chicago from his home in St. Louis, although it was less than three hundred miles away. Once when asked why he never cared to travel, He answered simply, "Why do I want to go anywhere. Everything I love is right here!"

John never ventured away from his home to see the world...but he brought the world to his home. He never missed the news shows and every morning he read the paper from front to back. He could answer any question about the economy, world conflicts, politics, baseball, football...and which store in town had Budweiser and Busch beer on sale.

John never made a lot of money but he was very successful. His criteria for success was to always have an extra case of beer on hand and good food to offer when friends came to visit.

John worked hard at making a living for his family. In his younger days he delivered furniture for a popular store in St. Louis. When he retired at 62, he was a shipping clerk. He had a strong back that supported a big heart. He was always willing to help anyone in need.

John loved life. The one word in his vocabulary that he used a lot, along with some very colorful language was the word, *beautiful*. That's how he looked at things. He brought something special to everyone he came in contact with; if it was a gloomy, rainy day, he reminded us how much the soil and trees needed the moisture. If it was clear and sunny, then it was *beautiful*.

John Ruskin was a poet. He looked beyond what he saw with his eyes...he always got to the heart of things. When others just saw a large stone building, John observed that it was a *beautiful* structure because it took skill and man-power to put it together. It was *beautiful*, not only for its looks, but because its construction put food on the table for many families.

When others saw a tree...it was only a tree, but to John it was a beautiful living thing that had a purpose. It provided shade on a warm day; it grabbed the white snow to create a *beautiful* picture in the winter. When its leaves would fall, it would fertilize the earth; its branches provided a home for the birds; and in due time it could be used for even more purposes, furniture, paper, wood for the stove. All these things meant jobs, and jobs meant people could feed their families.

There was never a family get-together that John wasn't surrounded by people. He drew them because he loved everybody. Something can be said of John Ruskin that cannot be said of many others, *John had no enemies*. His kindness, his tremendous sense of humor and his wonderful laughter filled the room. His family never had to look far to see where he was. He was invariably surrounded by people who felt better just because he was there.

John Ruskin was a happy man who wanted and prayed for everybody else to be happy too. And we all were, just because he was around.

John Ruskin was a grateful man. He never

stopped thanking God for all the things that most people take for granted. John took nothing, or no one for granted.

John Ruskin was not a boastful man...but he never missed a chance to brag about his family. When his only child, a daughter, was twelve and confined to Shriner's Hospital, for four months, he was only allowed to visit her one hour a week. Due to the polio epidemic, the children could only have visitors on Sunday afternoons from two to three. John was never one to break rules, he couldn't visit, but that didn't stop him from *seeing* her. Back then, John didn't have a car so he took two buses to get to the hospital just so he could sit out on the lawn and look at her through the long window that was next to her bed...and she never even knew he was there!

John Ruskin loved his grandchildren..he boasted about them always. "Look at 'em...ain't this a wonderful family?" he would say with pride.

John Ruskin felt God had truly blessed him when he was given eleven great-grandchildren. "Honest to God," he would ask, "Have you ever seen such *beautiful* kids?"

John Ruskin loved one woman, Annie Baker, in his life and he loved her with all his heart from the time they were teenagers through fifty seven years of marriage and to all eternity.

John Ruskin was often referred to as Big John...not so much for the size of his body, but for the size of his heart. John knew how to love and he was never embarrassed to tell anyone how much he loved them.

Big John had no prejudices...he was a good man who appreciated everything, and everyone around him. He saw God's work and God's plan in all of life's situations.

Perhaps the best tribute to John is to say that he always made each member of his family feel loved.

John's friends called him **"Big John."**

His wife called him, **"Johnny."**

His grandchildren called him, **"Pop."**

His great-grandchildren called him, **"Poppy."**

And thank you, God, I was privileged and so very, very blessed to call him, **"Dad."**

He was *beautiful!*

John W. Ruskin
August 18, 1910 - February 28, 1995

I HOPE, I HOPE, I HOPE,

There's this little fundamentalist church not far from my home and I think the pastor must frantically search through every old issue of Reader's Digest to come up with sayings to put on the marquee which is situated strategically on the front lawn so that it is almost impossible not to see it when taking the curve in the road. I'm certain this gentleman has a great sense of humor because very often his choice of sayings are quite humorous and you can't help but get a kick out of them. Occasionally, though, he comes up with something really profound, real food for thought. Such was the case very recently.

I'm certain it was the Holy Spirit who nudged me to take the route home that passed this little church after meeting my dear friend for lunch. And she is a dear friend to drop what she was doing to meet me knowing that I certainly hadn't been good company lately. Within the past eight weeks, I had lost my father and I miss him desperately, I lost my uncle, I lost an old friend, two more of my friends had been diagnosed as having cancer, and still another friend was in the process of undergoing chemotherapy. My mother had just been released from the hospital after giving us a terrible scare and a close member of our family was waiting to find out if he needed by-pass surgery. Suddenly, Job became my patron saint!

Although I had indulged my sadness by indulging my appetite for a greasy hamburger and fat-loaded chili...it didn't help. Now not only was I sad by the things I couldn't control, I was angry that I didn't control the things I could...me. Normally I would not have taken that particular route home, but almost without thinking, certainly not planning, I proceeded down the road that took me past the little church with the marquee. Still filled with a thousand, "Why, Lord?" questions, I looked up at the lettering wanting to be entertained more than inspired. Then it hit me. DEATH IS NOT A HOPELESS END, IT IS AN ENDLESS HOPE.

Wow!

I wanted to hug the pastor and thank the Holy Spirit, or visa versa. It dawned on me why I had been so consumed with so much grief. I had misplaced hope. (I would hate to think I ever lost it.) I also realized that it's okay to be sad when the circumstances warrant it as long as we don't lose hope. Without hope, sadness leads to depression and isolation until we find we are spending more time feeling sorry for ourselves than concern for others whose problems are far more immediate.

Perhaps *hope* is not totally appreciated in the secular world. The real meaning is obscured by the vernacular. There's a vast difference between, "There's hope that I'll lose ten pounds by summertime," in comparison to, "There's hope that death is not the end."

Certainly the madness and devastation in Oklahoma, Rowanda and Bosnia conjure up a thousand questions about why these things happen. We can never explain the hatred and evil in our world, but hope allows us to see beyond it. The horror of the crucifixion came before the joy of the Resurrection. Jesus' triumph over death and His promise of salvation give us hope.

Imagine the pain of the families of the victims in the Oklahoma bombing, especially the ones who suffered the loss of a child. Where can one go with that kind of grief...and where can you find consolation if you don't have hope?

By the time I pulled in my driveway, I had processed all the thoughts that I have just shared with you. These were facts that I had learned and believed in my religious education, but had not applied them in my grief.

Our Dear Lord knows how fickle our thoughts, and sometimes, our convictions can be so as an added bonus He allowed me a beautiful experience that same evening. Again, there was that gentle nudge by the Holy Spirit that moved me to call one of my friends, Carmelita, who had just finished another round of chemotherapy. My mother's illness had consumed a great deal of my time, but the few moments I set aside to inquire about Carmelita's progress with her treatments were never satisfied. Each time I tried to call her, there was no answer. I figured, "no news is good news" so I assumed that she was out and about. Not so. It seems that she had just returned from the hospital and her condition was rapidly declining. She was totally aware that she would die very soon so she called for a meeting with her husband and pastor and planned her funeral. Although her speaking was labored, her attitude was peaceful.

She shared with me how she wanted her funeral Mass to be joyful because that's how she looked forward to her death. Carmelita spoke about the wonderful reunion with her loved ones that she was looking forward to. She told me how much our friendship meant to her over the years and asked me to pray that her husband, an ordained deacon, would have the grace to work through his loneliness. She spoke about how her suffering had become such a tremendous means to grow in a closer relationship with Our Lord. She called attention to the fact that she had lived longer than the original prognosis had stated, so she referred to that time as her "grace period," that period of time she had received so much grace.

I'll always cherish that conversation with Carmelita, and I'll always be grateful to God for her friendship and her witness. She made the words on the marquee come alive. She was approaching her death, *not as a hopeless end, but as an endless hope!*

Things are going to be okay.

Part Three

Food for the Body...

by

Father Ken Roberts

Part Three

Food for the Body

Gary Ken Loberg

TASTE AND SEE

It seems appropriate to me to use this title for the section of this book devoted to food. The complete phrase is in Psalms 34:9, *Taste and see how good the Lord is...*

Perhaps each family should have a plaque in their kitchen or dining room with this phrase on it as a reminder of God's providence. Hopefully, we all remember to say grace before each meal and thank the Lord for all His gifts of food that too often we take for granted. When one considers the astounding number of people starving in the world, a simple meal is reason to rejoice and be grateful.

Meals are very important to family life, it's the time when all gather to share, not only the food on the table, but conversation. Families who make a point to share at least one meal together each day find they become more involved with each other. There's no doubt about it, meals are a very important time for families and it doesn't make much difference if the menu is considered gourmet quality, down home cooking, just soup and a sandwich, or a quick stop at your local fast food chain, the important thing is the togetherness. It's the sharing with one another.

172

Now, if the food is really good, the meal becomes a little more special. It sort of sets the mood for the mealtime.

Leisure is a commodity I don't seem to have much of, so consequently, I have never cultivated any hobbies, except cooking. Perhaps, it was the logical choice since we must eat and I love good food. Over the years I have tried many recipes (some failed) and even created some new dishes (some failed too) but I enjoyed the activity and eventually I became pretty at ease around a kitchen. When I find a dish I particularly enjoy, I want to share it with my friends who unfortunately are scattered across the country. I can't very well call them up and invite them for a meal, but when I'm in their area and they invite me for a meal, I like to ask if I may prepare it. By the way, I usually do this with friends I know well because I am not the neatest cook and if I fail at a new dish, they're quite understanding.

I have included many recipes from some of my friends who have prepared such wonderful meals for me. It is fitting to give them credit for their culinary arts so occasionally I have added a few notes about a particular dish that I think you will enjoy. And though I enjoy cooking I am a far cry from a gourmet, so many of these recipes are fast and simple and none call for ingredients other than what you are most likely to have on your spice rack.

If I had prepared this manuscript several years ago, the ingredients of the following recipes would have been loaded with real butter, lots of gravies and heavy sauces, even roast pork with crackling (the fat surrounding the cut of meat that is seared and *oh, so good*), but since I must answer to my cardiologist, I have altered the recipes to minimize the fat intake. Hopefully it still has flavor without being unhealthy.

Some may find it unusual that I have included recipes in a book that is classified as religious reading. Not at all. On the contrary, it is my attempt to share with you some things that I have enjoyed. Any of you who have heard me preach will know that the main focus of my ministry is on the Eucharistic Meal. And if we cultivate an appreciation for meals, the coming together to share with one another, we can grow in our appreciation for the Mass, the real Bread of Life!

ABOUT THE INGREDIENTS...

When choosing cuts of beef for the recipes that call for it, I suggest you pick the leanest cut and trim off any remaining fat. It's a fact that fat adds flavor, but it also boosts cholesterol and in general, it's downright unhealthy.

I recommend using boneless and skinless breasts of chicken to decrease the fat content and instead of regular table salt, you can use a salt substitute or *no-salt* herbs that are readily available in the spice section at your grocers.

Whenever the recipe calls for butter or margarine, you may use the low-fat spreads that are plentiful in the dairy section. Using skim milk instead of whole milk or cream is also advised as well as egg substitutes instead of whole eggs. Little flavor is lost and fat content is greatly reduced.

ENGLISH COOKING

"The British are coming, the British are coming..."

It's true, but I hate to admit it, that the British are not known for their culinary expertise. Nevertheless, you can't get fish and chips any where in the world that compares to England. Of course, I'm prejudiced...that is my native land. I also believe that English roast beef and Yorkshire pudding can't be served up any where like we had at home.

The British Isles are known for their ethnic dishes not so much by taste as by the unusual names, i.e., Bubble and Squeak, Toads in the Hole, Trifle, Shepherd's Pie, Welsh Rarebit, Crumpets, Scones, Marzipan, Yorkshire Pudding (which is really not a pudding) and Christmas Pudding (which also is not a pudding).

Allow me to translate. **Bubble and Squeak** is a traditional English dish usually made from left over cold cooked beef, thinly chopped, mixed with cold sliced thin cooked potatoes and finely chopped cabbage and other greens then fried. It gets its name from the sound while it is frying.

Toads in the Hole, is another favorite English dish prepared by placing cooked, browned sausages in a **Yorkshire Pudding** batter, then baking. (the recipe for Yorkshire Pudding is offered later in this section). The dish is usually served with gravy.

You can better understand why I chose the name **SHEPHERD'S PIE** for this book when you consider that it usually consists of left-over meat, chopped thinly and baked with a mashed potato topping. It takes what was used before and dresses it up in a new package!

Welsh Rarebit, also from the British Isles, is a popular dish primarily consisting of an egg and cheese mixture poured over toast. By adding dry mustard and a few spices, it becomes quite savory.

The British love their tea and **Crumpets** but I doubt if they are really served often because they have mostly been replaced by either cookies or English muffins which can be purchased at any store. Crumpets are not all that easy to prepare. It's a soft yeast cake baked on a griddle in special metal rings, then dried and toasted with butter. By the way, what you call "cookies" in the United States are called "biscuits" in England. And American biscuits are called "scones" over there.

I don't know where **Marzipan** got its name but it is an almond paste. To tell you the truth, I've never cooked with it, although my mother sometimes mixed it with a few other ingredients to create an icing for cakes.

When Americans taste **Christmas Pudding**, they invariably comment that it tastes like what you refer to as, fruitcake. The preparation of it is much different and just in case you want to have an English Christmas sometime, I included the recipe in the dessert section.

CHICKEN AND DUCK

BEER CHICKEN AND RICE

I was introduced to this dish years ago by Anna Marie Waters' family. The flavor is great and the preparation doesn't take very long. A new way to dress up chicken.

3 chicken breasts (halved to equal 6 pieces)
1 medium sliced onion
3 medium sliced carrots
2 tabls. of low-fat margarine
1 tabl. of chicken soup base (you can use the chicken bouillon crystals)
1 can of beer (non-alcoholic beer if you prefer...the flavor is the same in cooking)
1 heaping tabl. of flour
1/2 c. of water
pepper to taste
3 cups of instant rice prepared separately according to the directions on the box.

In a deep skillet (medium heat), melt the margarine and add chicken, sliced onion and sliced carrots. When the onion becomes clear, add chicken bouillon and a can of beer. Simmer on low heat for about an hour. Mix flour and water until smooth. Add to beer mixture and stir. Serve over rice.

CHICKEN BREAST AND STUFFING

If you're looking for a dish that's easy and tastes good enough for company, this is for you.

6 chicken breasts (halves)
1 box of stuffing mix prepared as directed on the box adding about 1/4 c. more water
1 egg or 1/2 carton of egg-substitute.

Grease a 9x13 glass baking dish with low-fat spread. Place chicken breast on bottom. Beat an egg or egg-substitute and fold into stuffing mix. Pour over chicken breasts and bake uncovered in a 350 degree preheated oven for about 45 minutes. Serve with a chilled can of cranberry sauce and your favorite vegetables. *It's a holiday taste treat you can serve in the middle of the week!*

CHICKEN AND MUSHROOM GRAVY

This dish is certain to delight the cook who loves to serve good food with little fuss.

2 chicken breasts (halved and sliced again to

to create 8 sections.
1 can of cream of mushroom soup
1 small sliced onion
2 teas. of chicken bouillon crystals
2 tabl. of low-fat margarine
1 12 oz. bag of egg noodles prepared as
directed on the package.

In a deep skillet, place chicken pieces and onion in melted margarine. When chicken is about done, add chicken bouillon and cream of mushroom soup, mix well. Simmer over low heat for about 20 minutes. Serve over egg noodles. *Great with just a simple salad.*

CRISPY DUCK ALA BOB

Bob and Emily Preuss from Chicago know how to serve up one of my favorite dishes. Emily gives Bob all the credit for his creativity and I give Emily credit for allowing Bob to experiment in her kitchen.

One 3 to 5 lb. duck
Clean duck thoroughly. Splash cavity with Cabernet Sauvignon wine. Sprinkle cavity with salt, pepper and thyme. Place a quartered orange in cavity and close with skewers.

Sauce:
1 c. Orange Marmalade
1/2 c. brown sugar

1 c. orange juice
3 tabls. corn starch
1 c. Cabernet Sauvignon wine
1/4 c. currant jelly

Combine all sauce ingredients in a 2 quart sauce pan and bring to a boil. Sauce will slightly thicken. Brush duck liberally with cooked sauce and roast uncovered on a covered charcoal grill by indirect method (drip pan placed under duck to catch fat and drippings - hot coals placed at sides of grill, away from drip pan). Add coals to each side as needed about every half hour. Baste duck often during cooking with sauce. Pierce fatty areas with fork to help drain off fat.

Cooking time: approximately two hours...until duck is tender and skin is crispy.

Suggested to be served with rice, asparagus and salad. *A real feast!*

BEEF

ROAST BEEF and YORKSHIRE PUDDING
(with brown gravy)

Certainly one of my very favorite dishes and the one that I most often prepare for my friends. This is probably the signature dish of the English. In our home, it was usually served with roast potatoes, Brussels sprouts and peas. If you want to serve a strictly English meal, this is the one.

This recipe will generously serve a party of six.

> One 4 to 5 lb. beef roast (I use boneless
> bottom round)

Wash the beef roast. Place in a roasting pan that has been prepared with a non-stick vegetable oil spray. Cover and place in a cold oven. then roast for approximately two hours at 350 temperature, remove cover and let brown for another 30 minutes. You might want to use a meat thermometer to insure the meat is cooked the way you prefer. Also, check often to make certain there is liquid at the bottom. You can add small amounts of water accordingly.

Yorkshire Pudding:

2 c. of flour
1-1/2 c. of milk
1/2 c. of water
4 well beaten eggs.
2 tabl. of margarine

Prepare your batter for the Yorkshire pudding by allowing all the ingredients (including the eggs) to become room temperature. Beat eggs until they become light, then gradually add small amounts of water, constantly blending at the medium dial on your electric mixer. After all the ingredients are combined, continue to use the mixer for about another two to three minutes.

Melt your margarine in a glass baking pan (13x9) in a hot oven (425). When margarine has turned to liquid and begins to bubble, immediately pour the batter into the hot pan and bake for approximately 30-35 minutes. *Watch it rise!*

Brown gravy:

1 c of liquid from roast beef
1 c. warm water
2 heaping tabl. of flour
1 teas. of beef bouillon crystals or beef base

Pour the remaining liquid from the pan used to roast the beef into a saucepan. (Add enough water if needed, to equal one cup of liquid)   Make certain fat is drained from the liquid.   At medium setting, add beef base to the liquid and heat, stir till blended. In a shaker jar, mix flour and warm water and shake for a couple of minutes. Pour gradually in saucepan, stirring constantly until mixture begins to thicken. Add small amount of water if needed. Add seasoning according to taste. (You may also add a couple of teaspoons of a commercial brown gravy preparation for color.)

Important: The Yorkshire Pudding must be served immediately from the oven...and don't be disappointed when you see it fall after a couple of minutes.   It's supposed to. The taste is still wonderful when you spoon the gravy over it.

Roast some potatoes your favorite way along with some buttered Brussels sprouts and some young tender green peas, and you're eating in style, English style.   CHEERIO!

SHEPHERD'S PIE

This is a great way to dress up that left-over roast beef and gravy.

Cut up cooked roast beef in small pieces, fry up some small chopped onion and mix both with a little bit of dried parsley and that left-over gravy. (If you don't have any left over, you can use a can of prepared brown gravy, enough to moisten the meat mixture making it juicy.) Mix together and pour in a deep casserole dish that has been sprayed with non-stick vegetable oil.

Prepare mashed potatoes your favorite way, and spread on top of the meat mixture. (It's best when you add some shredded cheddar cheese). Bake uncovered in a fairly hot oven for 25 minutes at 375.

If you would don't have any left-over roast beef, you can substitute the meat mixture with browned ground round (hamburger meat).

STEAK PIE

Originally prepared as 'steak and kidney pie' but this recipe is without the kidney. Organ meats are very high in cholesterol and preparing the kidney by first boiling it takes quite a bit of time and frankly, just the thought of it doesn't appeal to most Americans. If you're one of the brave souls who has no cholesterol problems, and you don't mind the inconvenience of preparing the kidney, just boil it for an hour, cut in small pieces and add to the recipe below.

1 beef round steak about 1/2 in. thick
2 tabl. of olive oil
1 medium chopped onion (apple size)
1 8 oz box of fresh sliced mushrooms
1/2 c. of dry red wine
1 tabl. of flour
1 c. water
Pie pastry

Salt and Pepper to taste.

Place oil in a hot fry pan. Add steak that has been cut into bite size pieces and rolled in flour. Brown stirring often. When meat is done add onion and cook until clear. Fold in mushroom. When mushrooms are done, add wine. Cover and let simmer for about 15 minutes. Mix flour and water. Shake well. Pour into meat mixture at medium heat and stir until it thickens. You may want to add some prepared brown gravy to darken the color.

Use a large deep-dish pie pan or shallow baking dish. Spread the pie pastry on the bottom and sides then pour in mixture. Top with another pie pastry. Make slits in the top pastry to allow for juice to bubble.

Place on a cookie sheet or large round pizza tin and bake at 400 or until top crusts begins to brown.

This is good served with creamed (or mashed) potatoes, and broccoli spears.

<u>EASY</u> SAUERBRATEN & POTATO PANCAKES

This is a favorite at the Eckenrodt household in St. Louis...with a name like that it's no surprise. Kathy has succeeded in mastering this traditional dish without all the mess, fuss, and time. Since Kathy is part Polish, maybe we could call this 'Polish Sauerbraten'? Ron doesn't mind as long as she prepares this family dish often and plenty of it!

> 3-4 lb. lean chuck roast (trim away extra fat)
> 1 large bay leaf
> 1/2 c. dark molasses
> 1/2 c. red wine vinegar
> salt and pepper to taste

Brown the chuck, both sides, on high heat. Simmer in enough water to cover the bottom of covered pan for about 30 minutes. Add flour, water, bay leaf, molasses, and vinegar and simmer for about two hours until tender. Gravy will thicken, add water according to your desired consistency.

> Potato pancakes:
> 4 medium size potatoes cut in quarters.
> 2 eggs, (or egg substitute)
> 1 tabl. of dehydrated onion
> 1/2 teas. parsley flakes
> 1/4 teas. sage
> 3 big tabl. flour.
> Low-fat vegetable oil for frying

Cut potatoes, 1/2 egg mixture and the remaining ingredients and put in blender. Set at medium speed until contents are grated and add remaining eggs. Blend. Pour in bowl.

In a fry pan with 1/8 to 1/4 in. of oil, drop batter (a gravy ladle full). Cook until brown on both sides. Turn once.

Sauerbraten and potato pancakes are great served with applesauce and cooked red cabbage.

187

CHILI

This recipe comes from Ann (Anna Marie) and Butch Waters. It's easy to prepare and perfect for a small meal in the chilly winter. Maybe ,we should call it, "Chili for when it's chilly". Maybe not...

2-1/2 lbs of ground chuck (to be really health conscious, substitute ground turkey)
2 medium chopped onions
1 small chopped green bell pepper
1 tabl. chili powder
2 teas. garlic powder
1 28 oz. can of chopped tomatoes
2 #3 (46 oz.) cans of chili beans in chili
    gravy.

Brown meat, add onions and pepper and simmer until onions are clear, add spices, tomatoes, and chili beans and cook on low heat for about an hour stirring occasionally.

Ann prepares a box of macaroni and cheese dinner according to package directions and mixes it in with about four to five cups of left-over chili for a quick dinner dish later in the week. Serve up a salad...and you have another full meal!

PORK

SMOTHERED PORK CHOPS

An easy, but tasty, dish Judy Horvath serves has to be included in some of my favorite meals. You can mix this up, push it in the oven, open a couple cans of carrots and peas, serve with applesauce and tossed salad and your guests will think you slaved away all day preparing this fare.

6 boneless butterfly pork chops (fat trimmed)
2 10 oz. cans of condensed cream of
   mushroom soup
2 c. uncooked rice
10 oz. of water
4 oz. of Chablis wine
1 4 oz. can of mushrooms (drained)
1 package of dry onion soup mix

Brown pork chops in a non-stick pan. Set aside. Mix the remaining ingredients together. In a 15x10 baking pan, lay pork chops on bottom, cover with mixture and bake in a preheated oven at 375 for one hour. Serves six.

SWEET AND SOUR PORK
WITH RICE

    This is a good change of pace entree that has a Polynesian flare. It's easy to prepare and very enjoyable.

    1 1/2 lb. of lean pork cut into bite size pieces
    1 can of chunk pineapple (20 oz.)
    1 large onion sliced in fairly large sections
    1 green pepper sliced in fairly large sections
    8 oz. of barbecue sauce (not smoky)
    3-4 cups of cooked rice.

Brown pork pieces in a deep frying pan. Drain fat when done. Add onion and green pepper and simmer on low heat until vegetables are cooked. Add barbecue sauce and pineapple with juice. Simmer for 30 minutes. Thicken and serve over warm rice.

FISH AND SEAFOOD

When I go to Louisiana, I always try to make time to visit with my old friends, Cyrille & Mabel Waguespack. They live in Cajun country and Mabel has mastered the art of Cajun cooking. I can always count on food that is unique. And yes, Mabel does serve, "Jambalaya, Crawfish Pie, and Filet Gumbo!"   Although I would love to share many of the recipes with you that Mabel has set before me, I think you would be hard pressed to acquire the ingredients. Crawfish is not plentiful except in that region. If you have ever had Crawfish bisque you know it is a dish difficult to come by any place else...besides being a lot of work. I have asked Mabel to send me a few of her recipes that contain ingredients that are accessible to all of the regions. The following are a few of my favorites.

SHRIMP JAMBALAYA

A rice cooker is recommended for this dish, and may I add, if you serve rice often, this is a great investment. There are many dishes that are prepared right in the cooker and they come out perfect every time. It's worth the investment. If you do not have a rice-cooker, you could try a slow cooker but I must admit I have very little experience with that appliance and I'm certain it would take longer to cook.

1 10 oz. can of beef broth
1 medium onion (chopped)
1 medium bell pepper (chopped)
1 4oz can of mushrooms drained
1 stick of melted low-fat margarine
1 lb. of shrimp peeled and scalded
2 1/2 c. of raw rice (cooker measurements)
        equal to 2 c. regular measurement
1 8oz c. of tomato sauce
Salt and Pepper to taste.

Wash rice, drain well. In an 8 or 10 cup rice cooker combine all the remaining ingredients, stir well and season to taste. Cook on 'cook' cycle and leave on warm cycle for 1/2 hour before serving. Do not double this recipe unless you are using a second cooker.

CRAB MEAT LANDRY

This is a beautiful dish with a special flavor. It's one to keep for those special occasions...or if you just want to serve the family a special treat, you'll love this recipe.

1 lb. of drained crab meat or imitation

crab meat cut in small bits
1 medium chopped onion
1/2 c. chopped celery
1/2 chopped bell pepper
1 stick (1/2 c.) of low-fat margarine
2 tabl. of mayonnaise
1/2 c. of evaporated milk
2 tabls. of cornstarch
1 c. mashed corn flakes
1/2 bread crumbs
Salt and pepper to taste

Preheat oven 350 degrees. Melt margarine in a sauce pan over medium heat, add onions, celery, bell pepper, saute for about 6 minutes. Add milk, mayonnaise, cornstarch to mixture, stir well, add crab meat and corn flakes, stir well. Pour in a prepared (sprayed with non-stick oil) baking dish and top with bread crumbs. Bake for 30 minutes.

ORANGE ROUGHY, MY WAY

Sorry, but I didn't know what else to call it. After I was told to change my eating habits, I experimented with this dish. I hope you like it.

3 orange roughy filets (app. 6 oz. each)
1 small onion
2 tabls. of low-fat margarine
1/2 lemon sliced thin
1/4 c. Chablis wine
Prepared fish fry mixture to roll fish (you

can purchase this in most supermarkets)

Pat the fish dry with a paper towel, roll in fish fry mixture. Melt margarine in a frying pan on medium heat. When margarine is melted, place the filets evenly in pan then add sliced onion. Cook for about 10 minutes then turn filets over, add lemon slices and wine. Simmer for about 20 minutes allowing most of liquid to diminish. Season to taste.

SHRIMP AND CORN SOUP

Another one of Mabel Waguespack's specialties...

> 1/3 c. vegetable oil
> 3 tabls. flour
> 1 med. chopped onion
> 1 small chopped green pepper
> 2 med. stalks of chopped celery
> 2 tabl. of parsley (dried is fine)
> 1 bay leaf
> 1 1lb. can of whole peeled tomatoes not drained
> 2 1lb. cans of whole kernel corn drained
> 3 quarts of water

Make a roux with oil and flour stirring constantly until light brown. Add onions, celery, bell peppers, cook for about 10 minutes, then add shrimp, tomatoes and corn, cook for ten minutes more, then add water and simmer for about one hour. Salt and pepper to taste. *Toss a salad, or make a little sandwich and you have a great lunch.*

VEGETABLES

BROCCOLI LASAGNA

This dish can serve as an entree or side dish. It's tasty and you can be certain you'll give this recipe out again and again. How it came about is interesting. The broccoli mixture was given to me as a hot dip, but I liked it so much, I altered it to accommodate a whole meal!

>2 16 oz bags of frozen chopped broccoli
>1 large chopped onion
>1 stick of low-fat margarine
>2 10 oz. cans of cream of mushroom soup
>1 1/2 teas. of garlic powder
>2 c. of grated cheddar cheese (use the low-fat cheddar cheese substitutes found in the dairy section)
>9 cooked lasagna strips.
>6 or 8 oz bag of slivered almonds.

Cook broccoli as directed on package. In a frying pan, melt the margarine and add chopped onion, simmer about 10 minutes. Add soup to mixture until blended, then add garlic powder. While stirring on a medium heat, gradually add cheddar cheese. Stir till cheese is melted in mixture. Fold in cooked, drained broccoli.

Spray a 13x9 baking pan. Spread three lasagna strips on the bottom of the pan and cover with third of the broccoli mixture. Repeat twice. (there should be three layers of lasagna noodles and mixture)

Sprinkle almond slivers on top and bake in a preheated oven at 350 for 30 minutes.

If you're trying to decide what to do with some of that left-over turkey or chicken, throw some in between the layers....it's delicious!

CREAMY MIXED VEGETABLE BAKE

Ann Ruskin, Anna Marie's mother, brings this vegetable dish to all the family gatherings because everybody loves it. She always uses low-fat substitutes in the ingredients without sacrificing flavor.

    1 16 oz. package of frozen mixed vegetables
    1 small chopped onion
    3 tabls. of low-fat margarine
    1/2 c of fat-free sour cream
    1/2 c of fat-free mayonnaise
    1 6-8 oz bag of grated cheddar cheese
        (use low-fat substitute)
    Topping:
    1 c. of crushed Hi-Ho crackers
    2 tabl. of low-fat margarine.

Cook mixed vegetables as directed on package. Drain and set aside. In a sauce pan, saute onions in margarine and allow to simmer until onions are done. In a bowl mix sour cream, mayo, and cheese then add the onion mixture followed by the drained mixed vegetables. Pour in a prepared baking dish.

Topping: After the margarine is melted in a sauce pan, mix in the crackers and allow to moisten. Then sprinkle over vegetable mixture. Bake in a preheated 350 oven for 25-30 minutes.

This is a rich side dish that can take the place of a starch or potato. Very good.

CAULIFLOWER BOUQUET

This is another of Ann Ruskin's contributions. She reserves this dish for company because it easily serves six to eight and it looks so pretty on the table. The best part is it's easy to prepare.

Whole head of fresh uncut cauliflower
1 16 oz. package of frozen peas
1 16 oz. bag of baby carrots (ready to eat)
2 c. of white sauce.
1 tabl. of dried chives (for sprinkling)
salt and pepper to taste.

Trim the coarse green leaves away from the cauliflower. Cut the extra thick white stem short enough so the whole head will lie flat. Drop the whole head in a large pot of boiling water, flowerettes side up. Cook until it becomes tender, but not soft. (You don't want the cauliflower to come apart).

Prepare the green peas as package directs while cauliflower is cooking. (Don't overcook)

Prepare the carrots by placing them in a quart of boiling water and cook till tender.

White sauce:
6 tabl. of melted low-fat margarine
6 tabl. of sifted four
2 c. of skim milk
1 teas. of onion powder.

Melt margarine in a pot over medium heat, add flour and mix thoroughly. Add milk gradually while vigorously stirring. Add onion powder. Bring to a boil. Reduce heat, cook one minute longer, stirring constantly. (yields 2 cups)

When all the vegetables are done. Lift the whole head of cauliflower from hot water making certain that it doesn't break apart. Place in the middle of a large round platter. Place drained cooked carrots around the bottom of the head. Add the cooked, drained green peas to the thick hot white sauce. Mix, then pour slowly over the cauliflower allowing it to fall evenly around the sides and rest on the carrots. Sprinkle dried chives on top (and a little paprika for color if you wish)...then serve.

Your guests will feel special with this special touch

ZUCHINNI PARMESAN

When I was trying to cut back on fat and calories I used this recipe as my main dish.

3 zuchinnis (large cucumber size)
1 medium onion sliced in strips lengthwise
2 tabl. of olive oil
garlic powder
1 c. of spaghetti sauce (use the meatless, low-fat sauce that comes in a jar)
1/4 c. of Parmesan cheese (Parmesan is a hard cheese that is low in fat)

It is best to choose the size zuchinni as recommended to avoid the seeds in the middle as you will find in large zuchinnis. Wash, trim away stem and other end. Scrub the peel, but leave it on. Slice about 1/4 inch thick.

In a large stove-top wok, rub the bottom and sides with olive oil and heat, then sprinkle generously garlic powder around the sides of wok. It will stick if the oil pan is hot enough. Put onions in and stir to allow them to rub the sides. When onions are almost done, add zuchinni and cook over medium to high heat, stirring to allow them to rub the sides. When zuchinni begins to become clear, add spaghetti sauce and mix well. Simmer for about five minutes on low heat then sprinkle Parmesan cheese on top. Cover. (If you don't have a lid, a cookie sheet or pizza pan does the job.) Turn off heat and allow to sit for about five minutes until the cheese begins to melt.

GRANDMA'S PRETTY VEGGIES

In this case, the 'grandma' is an old friend, Nora Schopp, and the 'pretty veggies' are fresh green beans and fresh carrots. Nora dresses them up with a few more ingredients then puts them on the stove and forgets about them...until it's time to eat, of course.

1 lb. of fresh green beans, cut in 2 inch pcs.
1 lb. carrots, peeled, and sliced in 3/4 in. pcs.
1 medium chopped onion
2 tbls. of low-fat margarine
1/2 c. ketchup
1 c. water
1 bay leaf
1 teas. sugar
1 tabl. of bacon bits
salt and pepper to taste

Combine all ingredients and cook slowly, stir occasionally until vegetables are cooked. Add small amounts of water as necessary for cooking to insure there is enough liquid in the pot and vegetables do not burn.

This is a dish that could easily be done in a slow cooker, providing you allow enough time. It works best if you set the dial on 'high' and allow a few hours cooking time. Stir occasionally.

DESSERTS

BANANAS FOSTER

This recipe is from Brennan's Restaurant on Royal Street in New Orleans. Thanks to Pip and Barbara Brennan, I have permission to share this dish with you. It's one that I often fix for friends and it always gets raves. Serve it on a special occasion and you'll be cooking gourmet style!

    4 tabls. butter or low-fat margarine
    1 c. of brown sugar
    1/2 teas. cinnamon
    4 tabls. of banana liqueur
    4 bananas cut in half (lengthwise) then cut in half again. (16 pieces)
    4 scoops of vanilla ice cream (low-fat's fine)
    1/4 c. of rum

Melt butter in an alcohol flambe pan (a shallow fry pan will do) Add sugar, cinnamon, brown sugar and stir to mix well. Heat for a few minutes then place the bananas in the sauce and saute until soft. Add rum and heat well. Tip pan and ignite the sauce: keep a circular motion to prolong the flame until it burns out. Serve over vanilla ice cream. Spoon the hot sauce from the pan over ice cream and bananas. *Delicious!*

CHRISTMAS PUDDING

I'm sure all of you have watched Dickens CHRISTMAS CAROL , and if you recall, there was much joy and emphasis put into the presentation of the Christmas Pudding. At our house, Mum, placed the pudding on a plate, poured brandy over it, set it aflame , and we all sang SILENT NIGHT while the flame burned out.

It's traditional to boil a silver coin (six pence or a shilling) and put it somewhere in the pudding. The one who gets the piece with the coin will have good fortune and prosper in the new year. After all, they already have a shilling!

I remember my first Christmas in St. Louis. I had become good friends with Anna Marie's whole family so I was invited for Christmas dinner. It was quite a gathering, her mother and father , aunts and uncles. Her children were still small and couldn't understand the big deal about this pudding thing. To accommodate everyone so we could all eat at the same time, she covered the ping pong table. It was great but we sat just a little low. The children were small and couldn't understand why there was such a big deal over the Christmas Pudding. They would have just as soon skipped that and get to the pumpkin pie with whipped cream. But Anna Marie, wanting to make me feel more like home, prepared a Christmas Pudding. She remembered the traditional coin which I had referred to as a 'penny'. So, she boiled a few pennies and put them in the batter.

We set the pudding aflame and sang SILENT NIGHT, and we all began to eat. (whether we liked it or not). Anna Marie announced that according to Father Ken, whoever got the penny would have good luck. Her father exclaimed, "Wait a minute...are you saying you put pennies in here?"

Anna Marie said, "Yes, it's tradition!"

John stated calmly, "Have you ever heard of 'copper poisoning?"

We all pushed away our plates and got out the pumpkin pie!

Oh well, it was a nice thought. (To tell the truth, I never much cared for Christmas Pudding...but it was tradition.)

When I was young, it was an important part of every Christmas. Mum prepared the batter and we all stirred the pudding and made a wish. This custom was even preserved when I was at the Beda College, an English seminary in Rome.

1/2 c. of sifted flour
1/2 teas. baking soda
1/2 teas. salt
1/2 teas. cinnamon
1/8 teas. nutmeg
3/4 c. raisins
3/4 c. currants
1/2 c. chopped citron

1/2 c. candied orange peel
1/4 c. chopped walnuts or pecans
3/4 c. large soft bread cubes
1 c. ground suet (my cardiologist won't like
  that!)
1/c c. brown sugar
2 well beaten eggs
1/4 c. brandy

In a bowl combine flour, baking soda, salt, cinnamon and nutmeg. Add fruits, nuts and bread crumbs. Blend in remaining ingredients. Mix well. Pour into a greased 6 cup mold. Steam in boiling water for 6 hours. Be certain to cover the bowl with tight fitting foil and add water as needed to prevent scorching.

Before serving, invert the pudding on a platter, pour brandy over the top and light. When serving, cover with RUM sauce.

RUM SAUCE:
1/2 c. butter
1 1/2 c. of confectioners sugar
dash of salt
1/2 teas. vanilla extract
1/2 teas. of rum

In a bowl, combine butter, sugar, salt and vanilla. Beat until fluffy. Stir in rum. Chill. Makes 1 1/2cups.

We have prepared vanilla pudding as directed on the package and added a teas. of rum flavored extract, then poured while warm but not yet set over the Christmas pudding.

TRIFLE

Very British...and a lot of work if you prepare this dessert the traditional way. I experimented a little and invented an easy recipe with the same good taste but far less work.

    6 short cakes (the round sponge cakes already packaged to use with strawberry shortcake)
    1 c. sherry or fruit juice if you prefer
    1 quart of strawberries sliced in half
    1 large package (calls for 3 cups of milk) of instant vanilla pudding
    Cool whip (lite) for topping.

Break up the short cakes into pieces and place in a deep casserole dish. Pour liquid and mix well. Let soak for a while. Add more liquid if needed to insure cakes are moistened. Set aside.

Clean strawberries and add some sugar to make a little juice. Mix well.

Fold the strawberries into the cake mixture. Prepare the vanilla pudding as directed on the package and pour immediately over the other ingredients. Don't mix, but use a spoon to create a few holes in the cake substance so the pudding can flow through.

Refrigerate. Wait for about 2 hours before serving. Serve with whipped topping.

PINEAPPLE-RICE DESSERT

For something a little different and so good, try this recipe from Ann Ruskin.   It serves four.

2 c. of cooled, cooked rice
1 sm. can of crushed pineapple drained.
1 sm. container of lite whipped topping
1/2 c. of chopped pecans
1/2 c. of shredded coconut

Mix rice, pineapple, pecans and coconut. Add whipped topping and blend. Spoon in parfait glasses and you have a great dessert fit for company.

PINEAPPLE BREAD PUDDING

This rich dessert is from Thelma Keller of Effingham, Ill.   Thelma, an octogenarian, still offers her expertise in the kitchen of her very fine restaurant at the Keller Ramada Inn.   She wants to maintain the high standard of cuisine she helped to institute. With her permission, we are sharing this dish with you.

2 scant cups sugar
1 stick of low-fat margarine
1 16oz can of pineapple chunks (drained)
2 eggs
1/2 c. milk
10 slices of bread, cubed
1/2 c. brown sugar

Mix sugar, margarine and eggs, and mix well. Stir in pineapple and add milk. Fold in the bread cubes. If the bread is very dry, add a little pineapple juice. Bake in a greased (or sprayed) 9x13 pan at 350 for 40-50 minutes. Sprinkle the top with brown sugar while hot.

Serve with warm fruit sauce made with any fruit juice of your choice, a small amount of lemon juice, and thickened with cornstarch.

BREADS

BEER BREAD

This is so incredibly easy, you'll make it over and over. (By the way, it is purely coincidental that the first dish from the first group of recipes also called for beer. Even if you don't like the drink, you must admit it, it does justice to cooking...and in this instance, baking!)

> 3 c. self-rising flour (you must use self-
>   rising flour...no substitutes
> 3 tbls. of sugar
> 1 egg
> 1 12 oz can of beer.

Combine flour, sugar and egg, mix well then add beer. Mix again and form into two loaves. Place into two buttered bread pans. Bake in a preheated oven at 350 for one hour.

IRISH SODA BREAD

I think Kathleen Long, founder of the Chicago Marian Center, makes one of the best

Irish breads I have ever eaten. She doesn't bother to measure...she's done it so often that she just throws in a little of this and a little of that and it always comes out perfect. My compliments. Who says the Irish and English don't get along?

> 4 c. of flour (not self-rising)
> 1 tsp. of salt
> 1 tsp. of cream of tartar
> 1 tsp. of bicarbonate of soda
> 2 tabls. of soft margarine.
> 1 c. of buttermilk (or you may take regular
>   milk and add a 1 tabl. of vinegar, mix well.

Sift the dry ingredients into a bowl and add the margarine. Stir a bit. Make a well in the center and mix in enough liquid to make a soft spongy dough. Turn on to a floured board and shape quickly into 2 round loaves. Place on a floured baking sheet and score 3 marks on each with a knife. Bake in a hot oven 400 for 30-40 minutes, until well risen, lightly browned and firm underneath.

EASY (really easy) PECAN ROLLS

I asked Mary Sue and Larry Eck for this great recipe to include in the book. I know they are very busy people, always racing to meet a deadline to get the Medjugorje Magazine to the printer. Mary Sue was gracious enough to take time out to fax the recipe to me. She probably supposed that I would edit her instructions, but I thought it better for you, the reader, to get the 'real flavor' of her directions. This way, if you don't enjoy the recipe, you gotta love the instructions!

TO THE READER: Don't try the first recipe below...use the corrected one at the end...please!

The fax:

Father, this recipe came to us from another couple, also up to their eyebrows in ministry, who remembered with longing the take-all-day-to-make pecan rolls like our grandmothers used to bake. (No, these rolls aren't as good - ministry does require sacrifice.)

<u>1 small package of FROZEN dinner rolls.</u>
(you know, the little balls of dough). You really are going to need about 17 of those little frozen dough balls for this recipe. Some packages come with 36 in it. You don't need that much unless you're going to double it and then of course, you'll need two pans. You can use half of the dough balls and save the other half for another time.

<u>1 4oz. package of butterscotch pudding</u>
 (regular only...don't get the instant or sugarless)
1 c. brown sugar
1/2 stick of butter
1/2 c. of pecans.
Place rolls (STILL FROZEN) in a 9x13 pan. (You could just use half of the dough balls and put them in an 8x8 square pan, but then you would

have to cut down on the other amounts...so it's really best to go with the 9x13 pan and use the whole recipe like it is up there.)

Sprinkle the pudding mix over the rolls and then the brown sugar. Dot with butter and pour the pecans over all. (You know, if you like cinnamon, you could mix in a teaspoon full in that dry pudding mix...that would probably be real good.)

Do all this RIGHT BEFORE YOU GO TO BED - it'll take ten minutes time at the most. Stick the pan in your UNHEATED oven and leave it there until morning. (six hours is best - - if you're in ministry you're used to no sleep anyway.) Don't touch the rolls. Just turn on the oven in the morning and bake at 350 for twenty minutes. (DO NOT PREHEAT). Remove from oven and place a greased or PAM-sprayed cookie sheet over the rolls and invert. ALLOW THE PAN TO SIT ON THE COOKIE SHEET UNTIL IT COOLS, so all the yummy caramel drips off. Enjoy.

(AND SHE HAD THE NERVE TO CALL THESE 'REALLY EASY'! PERHAPS SO, IF YOU CAN GET THROUGH THE DIRECTIONS...)

A few days passed and I received a phone call from Mary Sue. "Did you put that recipe in the book yet?"

I explained that I didn't get that far yet. (I knew it would call for the gift of discernment to understand it all!)

She continued, "Thank God. I decided to make the recipe and I don't think I measured right because by the time they got done cooking, I had this caramel gook running all over my oven...it just swelled up and dripped all over. What a mess!"

"It was probably because I used only 8 of those little frozen dough balls when I should have used 16 or 17...I don't know what I was thinking. Another thing...you can't let those things sit in that oven any more than six hours or they get big then they start to fall down. Anyway, I'm faxing you the 'revised' recipe and it's really good. I made them 'the right way' and our daughter and her kids just loved them. They really are delicious!"

So dear readers, here we go again...

EASY, REALLY EASY, (yeah, right) PECAN ROLLS

17 RHODES dinner rolls (half of package)
1 4 oz pack dry butterscotch pudding
   (regular only)
3/4 teas. cinnamon mixed in dry pudding
1 cup of brown sugar
1/2 stick of butter
1/2 cup of pecans.

Place frozen dinner rolls in a 13x9 greased pan. Sprinkle dry pudding mix over the rolls then the brown sugar. Dot with butter and pour pecans over all.

Let sit in an unheated oven overnight, then bake (do not preheat) at 350 for 25 minutes. Remove pan. Place PAM sprayed cookie sheet over rolls and invert. Let stand till cool so all the caramel drips on to the rolls. *Amen!*

Epilogue

Good luck with any recipes you decide to try. I hope that you will enjoy them in fellowship with your family and friends...but remember, the most important feast takes place each morning in your parish church, the Eucharistic Feast.

God Bless,

Fr. Ken

BIBLIOGRAPHY

The following articles were taken from the *Medjugorje Magazine*. For more information about this magazine, call 708-968-4684.

ASK   *Vol 3, #4*
Father Knows Best   *Vol 4, #3*
There is You Mother   *Vol 1, #1*
Mary Had a Little Lamb   *Vol 1, #2*
When I Grow Up *Vol 3, #2*
Whose Sins You Shall Forgive   *Vol 2, #4*
I Did It All For You   *Vol 2, #3*
Conversion Crash   *Vol 3, #3*
Suffer the Little Children   *Vol 4, #2*
Choices   *Vol 3, #1*
Wings of Faith   *Vol 6 #3*
The Devil Made Me Do It   *Vol 2, #2*
The Grace to Know Your Gifts   *Vol 8, #2*

All of Anna Marie Waters' articles and the following articles by Father Roberts were taken from *DEAR CHILDREN*, the bimonthly periodical from The Chicago Marian Center. For more information about this newsletter, call 312-973-0739

Relating Vol 3, #3
Judge Not Vol 3, #5
A Truly Holy Father Vol 3, #4
Apologetics or Apologies Vol 5, #3
SON-Bathing Vol 5, #1
Corpus Christi Vol 6, #3
Lord, If It Is You Vol 4, #1
A Reason to Believe Vol 5, #2
Don't Give Up, Just Give Vol 6, #1
Home for the Holidays Vol 4, #5
O.D.'d on O.J. Vol 6, #2
Crossroads Vol 6, #4

more by Fr. Roberts from Pax Tapes...

THE ROSARY with Meditation and Song
90 minute audio cassette - Father Roberts leads the fifteen mysteries, recited in its entirety and offers a meditation for each mystery. Familiar songs are sung before each decade.

OUR CATHOLIC FAITH
24 Lessons on audio and video cassettes, a complete course of instructions including a text highlighting the main points of each lesson, Scripture references to support the Church's teachings, and suggested topics for discussion.

PROUD TO BE CATHOLIC
Available on audio and video cassettes. Four complete talks: The Pope, The Sacraments, The Mass, and Mary.

...and many, many more topics on audio and video cassettes.

To obtain a catalog of Father Roberts' books and tapes, call for information: 314 838 5135 or write to: Pax Tapes, Inc.
P. O. Box 1059
Florissant, Missouri 63031